Historical Developmental Psychology

This book explores and underlines the thesis that developmental psychology cannot function fruitfully without systematic historical scholarship. Scientific thinking not only depends on empirical-analytical research, but also requires self-reflection and critical thinking about the discipline's foundations and history. The relevance of history was made especially clear in the writings of William Kessen, who analyzed how both children and child development are shaped "by the larger cultural forces of political maneuverings, practical economics, and implicit ideological commitments." As a corollary, he emphasized that the science of developmental psychology itself is culturally and historically shaped in significant ways. Discussing the implications of these insights in the book's introduction, Koops and Kessel stress that we need a *Historical Developmental Psychology.* In the book's following chapters, historians of childhood – Mintz, Stearns, Lassonde, Sandin, and Vicedo – demonstrate how conceptions of childhood vary across historical time and sociocultural space. These foundational variations are specified by these historians and by developmental psychologists – Harris and Keller – in the research domains of emotions, attachment, and parenting. This collection demonstrates the importance of bridging, both intellectually and institutionally, the gap between the research of historians, and both current and future research of developmental psychologists.

This book was originally published as a special issue of the *European Journal of Developmental Psychology.*

Willem Koops is Distinguished Professor of Foundations and History of Developmental Psychology and Education at Utrecht University, the Netherlands. He is the Editor of the *European Journal of Developmental Psychology.* He is a Fellow of the American Psychological Association, the Association for Psychological Science, and the International Society for the Study of Behavioural Development (ISSBD).

Frank Kessel is Emeritus Professor at The University of New Mexico, Albuquerque, USA, where he was in the College of Education's Early Childhood Multicultural Education Program and a Senior Fellow in the Robert Wood Johnson Foundation Center for Health Policy. Previously, he served for twelve years as Program Director of the Culture, Health and Human Development Program at the Social Science Research Council, New York City, USA. He is also a Fellow of the American Psychological Association, the Association for Psychological Science, and the ISSBD.

Historical Developmental Psychology

Edited by
Willem Koops and Frank Kessel

Routledge
Taylor & Francis Group
LONDON AND NEW YORK

First published 2019
by Routledge
2 Park Square, Milton Park, Abingdon, Oxon, OX14 4RN, UK

and by Routledge
52 Vanderbilt Avenue, New York, NY 10017, USA

First issued in paperback 2020

Routledge is an imprint of the Taylor & Francis Group, an informa business

British Library Cataloguing-in-Publication Data
A catalogue record for this book is available from the British Library

ISBN 13: 978-0-367-58290-6 (pbk)
ISBN 13: 978-1-138-39420-9 (hbk)

Typeset in Myriad Pro
by codeMantra

Publisher's Note
The publisher accepts responsibility for any inconsistencies that may have arisen during the conversion of this book from journal articles to book chapters, namely the possible inclusion of journal terminology.

Disclaimer
Every effort has been made to contact copyright holders for their permission to reprint material in this book. The publishers would be grateful to hear from any copyright holder who is not here acknowledged and will undertake to rectify any errors or omissions in future editions of this book.

Contents

Citation Information

The following chapters were originally published in the *European Journal of Developmental Psychology*, volume 14, issue 6 (November 2017). When citing this material, please use the original page numbering for each article, as follows:

Introduction

Developmental psychology without positivistic pretentions: An introduction to the special issue on historical developmental psychology
Willem Koops and Frank Kessel
European Journal of Developmental Psychology, volume 14, issue 6 (November 2017) pp. 629–646

Chapter 1

Why history matters: Placing infant and child development in historical perspective
Steven Mintz
European Journal of Developmental Psychology, volume 14, issue 6 (November 2017) pp. 647–658

Chapter 2

Children and emotions history
Peter N. Stearns
European Journal of Developmental Psychology, volume 14, issue 6 (November 2017) pp. 659–671

Chapter 3

Emotion, imagination and the world's furniture
Paul L. Harris
European Journal of Developmental Psychology, volume 14, issue 6 (November 2017) pp. 672–683

Chapter 4

Putting attachment in its place: Disciplinary and cultural contexts
Marga Vicedo
European Journal of Developmental Psychology, volume 14, issue 6 (November 2017) pp. 684–699

Chapter 5

Attachment histories and futures: reply to Vicedo's 'Putting attachment in its place'
Robbie Duschinsky, Marinus Van Ijzendoorn, Sarah Foster, Sophie Reijman and Francesca Lionetti
European Journal of Developmental Psychology, DOI: 10.1080/17405629.2018.1502916

Chapter 6

On the history, present, and future of attachment theory: Reply to Robbie Duschinsky, Marinus van IJzendoorn, Sarah Foster, Sophie Reijman & Francesca Lionetti, 'Attachment histories and futures.'
Marga Vicedo
European Journal of Developmental Psychology, DOI: 10.1080/17405629.2018.1502920

Chapter 7

Cultural and historical diversity in early relationship formation
Heidi Keller
European Journal of Developmental Psychology, volume 14, issue 6 (November 2017) pp. 700–713

Chapter 8

Authority, disciplinary intimacy & parenting in middle-class America
Stephen Lassonde
European Journal of Developmental Psychology, volume 14, issue 6 (November 2017) pp. 714–732

Chapter 9

The parent: A cultural invention. The politics of parenting
Bengt Sandin
European Journal of Developmental Psychology, volume 14, issue 6 (November 2017) pp. 733–746

Notes on Contributors

Robbie Duschinsky is Director of Studies in Sociology at Sidney Sussex College, Cambridge, UK. His two major research interests are the development and contexts of mental illness and the use of qualitative methods within primary care research. He has also published widely in the sociology of childhood and the family. Robbie is a member of the Wellcome Trust Expert Review Group for Medical Humanities, London, UK.

Sarah Foster is a Graduate Tutor in the Department of Social Work and Communities at Northumbria University, Newcastle upon Tyne, UK. Sarah's research interests include attachment theory and its relevance to clinical and social work practice. Sarah teaches attachment theory and other psychological and sociological concepts to students pursuing Social Work, Guidance and Counselling, and Early Years Studies degrees.

Paul L. Harris is Professor of Education at Harvard Graduate School of Education, Cambridge, USA. He is interested in the early development of cognition, emotion, and imagination. His research interests include child development, cognitive development, emotional development, and language development. He is associated with the British Academy, London, UK; The Scientific Advisory Board, Arlington, USA; and the American Academy of Arts and Sciences, Cambridge, USA.

Marinus Van Ijzendoorn is Full Professor of Child and Family Studies at Leiden University, the Netherlands. His work focuses on the social, psychological, and neurobiological determinants of parenting and child development, with special emphasis on attachment, emotion regulation, differential susceptibility hypothesis, and child maltreatment.

Heidi Keller is Professor of Psychology in the Department of Human Sciences at the University of Osnabrück, Germany. Her main interest concerns the conception of development as the interface between biology and culture. Her research program concerns cultural analyses of infants' early socialization contexts and their developmental consequences in different cultural environments.

Frank Kessel is Emeritus Professor at The University of New Mexico, Albuquerque, USA, where he was in the College of Education's Early Childhood Multicultural Education Program and a Senior Fellow in the Robert Wood Johnson Foundation Center for Health Policy. Previously, he served for twelve years as Program Director of the Culture, Health and Human Development Program at the Social Science Research Council, New York City, USA. He is also a Fellow of the American Psychological Association, the Association for Psychological Science, and the ISSBD.

Willem Koops studied psychology at University of Groningen, the Netherlands, and during 1971–1981, he was attached to this University as Assistant and Associate Professor of Developmental Psychology. He gained his PhD at Groningen in 1980 and then moved to the Vrije Universiteit Amsterdam, the Netherlands as Professor of Developmental Psychology (1981–2002). He held the position of Dean of the Faculty of Social Sciences at Utrecht University during 2002–2012. Koops has published more than 60 (edited) books and special issues and over 300 papers in scientific journals, encompassing (early) social and cognitive development, the development of aggression and antisocial development, and studies on the history of childhood.

Stephen Lassonde is Director of The Ruth & Harold Newman Office of Prestigious Scholarships & Fellowships in the Hunter College at City University of New York, New York City, USA. Previously, he held the appointment of Dean of Student Life and Lecturer in History at Harvard University, Cambridge, USA.

Francesca Lionetti is a Visiting PhD Student at Queen Mary University of London, UK. She is associated with the following scientific bodies: European Association for Developmental Psychology, International Society for the Study of Behavioural Development, Society of Emotion and Attachment Studies, and International Association of Applied Psychology.

Steven Mintz is a leading authority on families, children, youth, and the life course. He has also published extensively on slavery, social reform, ethnicity, and film. For five years, he served as Founding Director of The University of Texas System's Institute for Transformational Learning, Austin, USA, which was responsible for designing and testing new educational models and technologies with the aim of making education more accessible, affordable, and successful.

Sophie Reijman is Research Associate within the Applied Social Science Group in the Department of Public Care and Primary Health at the University of Cambridge, UK. After studying at the University of Valencia, Spain, she obtained a Bachelor of Arts degree in Psychology at Leiden University, the Netherlands, and she holds a Master of Science in Developmental Psychopathology and a PhD in research cluster child maltreatment from the Centre for Child and Family Studies at Leiden University, the Netherlands.

Bengt Sandin is Faculty Member in the Department of Thematic Studies and also in Child Studies at Linköping University, Sweden. His approach concerns the amalgamation of technology and the humanities to increase understanding for and to find solutions to important future questions.

Peter N. Stearns previously taught at Harvard University, Cambridge; The University of Chicago; Rutgers University, New Brunswick; and Carnegie Mellon University, Pittsburgh (all in USA). He was educated at Harvard University, Cambridge, USA. He has published widely in modern social history, including the history of emotions, and in world history and has authored or edited over 135 books, mainly in social history and world history.

Marga Vicedo is interested in the history and philosophy of genetics, evolution, and animal research in the twentieth century. She is also interested in how ideas from biology are used in other fields such as psychology and the social sciences. In the Philosophy of Science, she has worked on scientific realism and the question of whether our best scientific theories offer us a reliable account of the world.

INTRODUCTION

OPEN ACCESS

Developmental psychology without positivistic pretentions: An introduction to the special issue on historical developmental psychology

Willem Koops and Frank Kessel

ABSTRACT

Emphasizing the importance of understanding children and child development as 'cultural inventions', William Kessen urged developmental psychologists to forego 'positivistic dreaming'. The first section of this paper summarizes Kessen's central ideas. In the second section the pretensions of positivism (classical nineteenth century positivism as well as twentieth century neo-positivism) are analyzed. The core critique of positivism is based on Poppers falsificationism and the so-called *Positivismusstreit* within the *Frankfurter Schule*. Despite those and related fundamental critiques, anti-positivism (such as Kessen's) does not imply anti-empiricism. One corollary – Although contemporary developmental psychology is dominated by empirical-quantitative approaches, a wider range of philosophical and methodological approaches are called for if the failings of lingering positivism are to avoided. In particular, twenty-first century developmental psychology requires critical thinking about the discipline's foundations and history, along with deep analyses of how childhood and child development, and the field itself, are historically and culturally embedded (as Kessen asserted). Section 4 concludes with several critical notes regarding, e.g., the predominantly Western orientation of historical studies of child development and the need to recognize the unavoidable normative, moral dimension in the study of human development. The final section provides a brief overview of the papers that comprise this special issue on historical developmental psychology.

1. Introduction

The often-cited developmental psychologist William Kessen (1925–1999) considered the American child a 'cultural invention' (Kessen, 1979). *Inter alia*, this implies that developmental psychology cannot function fruitfully without historical analysis. And that is what this special issue seeks to demonstrate.

The first section of this introduction focuses on Kessen's ideas. The second section takes a closer look at the meaning of 'positivism', a concept and movement Kessen often considered. In particular, we will assert that it is possible to be an anti-positivist while simultaneously believing that theoretical conceptions must be approached systematically and assessed empirically-analytically as rigorously as possible. In other words, while recognizing - as Kessen did later in his career - that scientific knowledge is always contingent on time and place, scholarly concepts and claims must remain open to empirical inquiry. Conversely, section three elaborates on the view that scientific thinking not only depends on empirical-analytical research, but also requires self-reflection, in particular, critical thinking about a discipline's foundations and history. Section four concludes with several critical notes as a bridge to brief descriptions of the papers that comprise this special issue.

2. Kessen's plea

During the (only) 'International Year of the Child' (1979), Kessen wrote an influential essay on 'The American Child and Other Cultural Inventions' (Kessen, 1979; also Kessel & Siegel, 1983). Among several other central observations Kessen pointed out that:

> No other animal species has been cataloged by responsible scholars in so many wildly discrepant forms, forms that a perceptive extraterrestrial could never see as reflecting the same beast. (Kessen, 1983, p. 27)

Understandably scientists who study children wish to continue to pursue what Kessen referred to as a 'positivistic dream', in which such multiple variations in the definition of *the* child are considered the 'removable [correctible] error of an [as-yet-]incomplete science' (l.c.). Kessen's view, however, was that developmental psychologists needed to finally attempt to bridge what he considered the abyss of the positivistic nightmare. This requires them to recognize that the upbringing and development of children, *as well as the sciences of developmental psychology and pedagogy*, are culturally-historically influenced in significant ways:

> For not only are American children shaped and marked by the larger cultural forces of political maneuverings, practical economics, and implicit ideological commitments (a new enough recognition); child psychology is itself a peculiar invention that moves with the tidal sweeps of the larger culture in ways that we understand at best dimly and often ignore. (Kessen, l.c.)

Grounding his position in historical analysis, Kessen suggested that, in the mid-nineteenth century, the United States of America was being prepared, socio-culturally, for the birth of what came to be known as child psychology. Against the background of the industrial revolution, he discussed three cultural-historical changes that have shaped the fundamental principles of developmental psychology through to the present. And while Kessen consequently spoke about *American* child and developmental psychology, his critique applies to *Western culture as a whole*, if only because of the dominant influence of North American developmental psychology in the twentieth and even twenty-first century. He did, therefore, delete the adjective 'American' (from the title 'The American Child and Other Cultural Inventions') in his revisited version in 1983; hence: 'The Child and Other Cultural Inventions' (Kessen, 1983).

In Kessen's analysis, the first cultural-historical change that led to the invention of the modern-day child was the gradual division between the domains of work and family. When women in America between 1830 and 1840 were excluded from the industrial workforce, this division, marked by the walls of the family home, became increasingly impregnable (Kessen, l.c., p. 31). Work was carried out in specialist workplaces (factories) by specialist people (men), and home became a place where one did *not* work.

Second, masculinity and femininity were so strongly separated that two different worlds arose: the 'ugly aggressive, corrupting, chaotic, sinful and irreligious' world of men and the 'sweet, chaste, calm, cultured, loving, protective and godly' world of women (Kessen, l.c.). This division made women 'naturally' and exclusively responsible for the upbringing of and caring for children.

A third change followed from the other two: As children no longer had access to the grown-up professional world and home 'took on the coloration of mother, hearth and heaven' (Kessen, l.c.), children became *sentimentalized.* They were seen as pure, unspoiled, and even 'heavenly'. Wordsworth's 'Heaven lies about us in our infancy' succinctly expresses this view (Stassijns & van Strijten, 2004, pp. 138, 139). Moreover, the critical importance of early childhood for lifetime development was canonized. Again, Wordsworth is (too) often quoted: 'The Child is father of the Man' (l.c. pp. 128, 129).

Kessen's central message is that these cultural foundations of 'developmental science' are generally not recognized as such, i.e., as culturally-historically contingent, and are often even regarded as fundamental laws of nature. As Kessen argued, in developmental psychology the importance of a harmonious family, the significant role of mothers, and the decisive role of early experience in the development of the child are conventionally considered as principles anchored in the laws of nature, for which researchers seek and find empirical evidence. And the now commonplace use of 'developmental *science*' can be seen as a final integration of developmental psychology with 'science', and not with the humanities. As a key qualifying corollary, this view overlooks, or at least tends to overlook, any and all alternative conceptions of the child and of development in different historical epochs and socio-cultural contexts. To Kessen, this also means that progress in developmental psychology, i.e., seeking deeper understanding of human development, cannot be achieved by collecting more and more empirical data but, also and as important, has to entail analyzing the basic principles and processes of the field from a cultural-historical perspective (again, as the title of his essay so precisely states: 'The [American] Child and *Other* Cultural Inventions'.

To provide a preview of the final sections below – Working within such a philosophical framework, the authors of the papers in this special issue are focused on a particular task: Providing various insightful illustrations of a critical cultural-historical approach to the ('fundamentals' of) developmental psychology.

3. Positivistic and empirical-analytical approaches

As signaled above, in Kessen's view the positivist program was and is fundamentally misguided; he therefore criticized 'positivistic dreaming', *viz.*, the assumption that empirical-experimental (human and social) science will yield fundamental facts and universal, timeless principles. Given that the terms positivism and positivistic have long been used by critics of 'normal science', examining them further is warranted. In the next subsection, the origin and meaning of the concept of positivism will be discussed, as well as a number of its characteristics that have been subject to criticism and that, therefore connect to the core of Kessen's position.

As a prefatory note, it is important to underline that the assumptions and goals of positivism can be rejected without implying an opposition to empirical research (as some movements in psychology and pedagogy antithetical to empirical science have asserted). Thus neither Kessen nor we are opposed to systematic and reflective empirical research in (developmental) psychology and pedagogy. On the contrary, whenever possible, and while acknowledging limitations on the possibility of data-collection and certainty of related interpretation, researchers should analyze and reflect on their theoretical assumptions in the context of the most systematic available empirical data. Such a principled stance of vulnerability, or humility, regarding the limits of scientific knowledge – which can be traced back, among others, to the philosopher of science Karl Popper (1902–1994) – will be referred to as an *empirical-analytical approach.*

3.1. The positivist approach

Positivism is the notion that only the empirical sciences can yield valid knowledge. Positivism asserts that science is solely based on empirical facts and rejects all metaphysical assertions and assumptions. The classical positivism from the nineteenth century merges with the *belief in the progress of the Enlightenment*, i.e., progress in science will eventually provide solutions to all possible problems (Steel, 1989, p. 99). Positivism emerged from the confrontation of philosophy with the successful modern (physical) sciences and the consequential view that the certain knowledge of empirical science could not be matched by philosophy (or the humanities in general). Already by the end of the eighteenth century philosophy had begun to cede the field of nature to positivistic modern physics and chemistry. And in the nineteenth century the humanities were also gradually redefined as empirical sciences. Positivistic sociology appeared first, promoted by Auguste Comte (1798–1857), considered the 'father of positivism' (Bourdeau, 2011); he referred to sociology as 'social physics' (Steel, 1989, p. 98). Comte's positivistic program for sociology was elaborated by his pupil Émile Durkheim (1858–1917).

In the case of psychology, the establishment of the first psychology laboratory by Wilhelm Wundt (1832–1920) in Leipzig (in 1879) has conventionally been identified as the beginning of positivistic, i.e., scientific, experimental psychology (Boring, 1950; as the canonical source). But here it is especially worth noting that critical historians have demonstrated how such accounts completely neglected the other deep dimension of Wundt's work (1900–1920), *viz.*, his *Völkerpsychologie* studies of phenomena such as language, art, myths and religions, law, culture in historical perspective, and more. (See, e.g., Blumenthal, 1977; Danziger, 1979; Leary, 1979) And it is plausible to see the spirit of the 'other Wundt' expressed in the various, emerging-in-the-1990s and now-vibrant forms of 'Cultural (Developmental) Psychology', for example, in the rich, paradigm-defining writings and research of Michael Cole (1996), Barbara Rogoff (2003) and Richard Shweder (1994). (See also Goodnow, Miller, & Kessel, 1995).

Comte's positivistic program of principles was described in his writing about the positive mind (Comte, 1844). That program also demonstrates the strong belief in progress that was intertwined with Comte's positivism. He believed, for instance, that the rise of the modern sciences was a slow but *inevitable* process. He formulated the *law of the three stages*: First, a theoretical stage when the explanation for phenomena is sought in supernatural powers. This is followed by humanity entering a metaphysical stage when the world is explained by referring to abstract principles or essences. Eventually humanity enters a positive stage when it becomes clear that only empirical science can yield real knowledge. At this stage knowledge should be considered as accessible to all and relevant for all daily requirements and needs. Therefore, according to Comte, positivism is *inevitable*. The law of the three stages is founded on the presumed positivistic law of progress and evolution of human thinking. Delanty and Strydom (2003, p. 14) have extensively described positivism. Assuming access to their writing, we will now further concentrate here on some criticisms of positivism by way of a discussion of Popper's ideas and the debate within the *Frankfurter Schule*.[1]

Positivists believe that scientific knowledge originates primarily via induction: By systematically observing specific perceptible phenomena one induces general and abstract laws. This, however, is not how it appears to unfold in scientific reality. A fundamental criticism of such a position came in the form of

[1]A detailed discussion of all these ideas, and those in the previous section, is contained in Koops (2016), notably chapter 1.

Popper's falsificationism (Popper, 1935, 1959) and his classic 'Even if one has seen a hundred white swans, the next one could still be black'. According to Popper, one can only falsify or refute, not ever confirm or prove a posited hypothesis. So 'all swans are white', can only be refuted by encountering a black swan. It follows then that one must first posit a certain assumption (hypothesis or H_1) and then try to refute it by rejecting the contrary hypothesis (H_0). And even if this succeeds, the basic hypothesis (H_1) can only be maintained *provisionally*, and never be lifted to the level of absolute knowledge through observation alone. For Popper, then, there is no pure induction from observation to certain knowledge.

Popper's description of this logical asymmetry between verification and falsification – hence *Conjectures and Refutations* (1963) – is a key element in his philosophy of science. It led him to choose falsifiability as the criterion to distinguish science from non- or pseudo-science: A theory can only be genuinely scientific if it is falsifiable. Falsifiability as a demarcation criterion for the distinction between science and *un*-science therefore led him reject the claims to scientific status of both Marxism and psychoanalysis, given that both theories are not falsifiable.

In summary, Popper made it clear that induction from observation cannot lead to true, universal knowledge, *and* that all scientific knowledge is temporary and provisional. This is a significant qualification of original positivist pretensions. Popper's analysis also seriously undermined the notion of inevitable progress. As a consequence, those following Popper's analysis have little reason to believe that scientific knowledge automatically advances and improves; they also do not have any reason to expect that we will ever be able to solve all social problems purely through knowledge derived via positivistic science. In addition, classical positivism's assumption that knowledge can be exhaustive and that induction one day will have yielded all important certainties about the universe is, for Popper, an indefensible optimism.

A complementary set of ideas emerged in the 1960s, in the form of a debate in Germany that became known as the '*Positivismusstreit*' (the Positivism battle); this exchange deepened the critique on positivism. (See Adorno, Albert, & Dahrendorf, 1993; Dahms, 1994) Even though it focused primarily on the methodology and epistemology of sociology, the debate was particularly relevant to positivist claim that science is value-free. The discussion between Theodor Adorno (1903–1969) and Popper, in particular, focused on this topic. It is noteworthy that both agree that the scientific practitioners are always embedded in cultural history and that their minds, therefore, are pervaded or shaped by this context. According to Popper, however, the ensuing scientific research is meant precisely to determine empirical-analytically the tenability of the claims of the embedded scientific researcher.

For their part, the philosophers of the so-called *Frankfurter Schule*, with key representatives such as Adorno and Jürgen Habermas (born in 1929), believed that although society as a whole could be analyzed scientifically, value-freedom was an illusion in *all* respects. The members of the *Frankfurter Schule* built on the theories of Marx, Hegel, and Freud (as noted, all unscientific in Popper's view). The fundamental assumption of the was that they could understand the structure of society as a whole and, in principle, identify the conditions to change or entirely alter this structure consistent with certain value assumptions. This approach was thus called *Critical Theory.* (In the 1960s and 1970s, widespread social criticism from the democratization movements, particularly at universities, was inspired by the *Frankfurter Schule* publications.)

The discussions that emerged during the *Positivismusstreit* made it clear that the value-freedom as claimed by positivism should at least be qualified. Such an analysis underlines that scientific researchers are members of a community whose work is shaped by the wider society's values. As a key corollary, these values play a role in their theoretical and methodological choices and commitments. For his part, Popper thought that falsificationism would provide the critical means to subject the tenability of theoretical claims to empirical-analytical test; and that, in turn, could always lead to the refutation of the claims. And the *Frankfurter Schule* believed that they could understand and modify social value patterns and dynamics. However, contrary to classical positivism's assumption that objective observations and logical induction guarantee value freedom, both did not deny – indeed, acknowledged – that values play a role in science. While Popper aimed to subject value-laden theoretical notions to scrutiny via falsificationism, the *Frankfurther Schule* sought to respond 'critically' to these values.

As a final note in this section, it is worth emphasizing that the account above is an abbreviated, selective account of the critique of positivism. Among other strands (emerging especially in the 1960s): Thomas Kuhn's analysis of scientific 'paradigms' and 'revolutions', and Michael Polanyi's discussion of 'personal knowledge' and 'the tacit dimension' (See Kessel, 1969).

3.2. The empirical-analytical approach

Whereas Adorno (1993) invented the term 'Positivismusstreit', Popper objected to the term as he did not want to call himself a positivist. Or, more accurately, he objected being considered (even) a *neo-positivist.*

Neo-positivism had originated during the period of the *Wiener Kreis*. The *Wiener Kreis* (1920–1938) referred to a group of philosophers and scientists who gathered around Moritz Schlick (1862–1936). Key figures included the economist Otto Neurath (1882–1945), and the philosophers Friedrich Waismann (1896–1959) and Rudolf Carnap (1891–1970). Often present but not a formal member of the group, Popper deviated from key points of the logical positivism or logical empiricism promoted by the group. Rejecting metaphysics and epistemology as useless, the Wiener Kreis sought to unify science by making use of a common scientific language, symbolic logic. Eschewing such a common core language, Popper described his own approach as *critical rationalism*. The term 'critical' is rather ambiguous: The Frankfurter Schule uses it to refer to *social criticism*; Popper wished to (*critically*) determine which theories were tenable and which were not.

Thus Popper criticized both classical positivism and the neo-positivism of the *Wiener Kreis*. Contrary to the positivistic tradition, he believed that all science is partial (and always incomplete); that scientific knowledge does not automatically advance but often has to take apparent detours; and that science cannot ever produce complete understanding and the solution of all social issues. He also agreed with the *Frankfurter Schule* that the theories and hypotheses of a scientist are can never be value-free in the sense that they are unconnected with the everyday lived environment (of the scientific community). But contrary to the *Frankfurter Schule*, Popper deemed it possible to refute untenable assumptions and hypotheses via falsification, not as in the tradition of positivism via induction. In essence, his falsificationism is an empirical-analytical tool: It aims to examine and refute hypotheses and predictions by making use of empirical data.[2]

Conducting path-breaking empirical-analytical research on infants, Kessen in fact established his reputation in the American behaviorist tradition, a paradigm that more than any other institutionalized positivist assumptions in mainstream psychology.[3] He was thus certainly aware of the importance of the empirical-analytical tradition. Later in his scholarly career, however, and based in part on his own study of historical sources (Kessen, 1965), Kessen sought to understand how the practice of developmental psychology and of theorizing in general was linked to the cultural history in which it was, and is, embedded. For him, and us, such self-critical understanding is the only way to preclude assumptions and views about children that are, as Kessen underlined, variable across cultural space and historical time being mistakenly considered natural, universal phenomena.

In a related vein, we suggest that scientific questions can only be answered in a meaningful way at the level of organization of the phenomenon being studied. We borrow this conception of 'level of organization' from the Dutch psychologist, Johannes Linschoten (1964). In a distinctive way, he made clear that questions at one level of organization cannot be answered by data at a different level of organization, at least not without losing relevance and understanding. As a

[2]Such an empirical-analytical approach remains a core element of the methodology of contemporary psychology. To give an example, in the second half of the twentieth Century Dutch (and European) psychology was totally redefined by De Groot's classic book (1961; English translation 1969), whose prescriptive methodology was largely based on the ideas of Popper. (See Busato, 2014 for a description of the effect of De Groot's work.).

[3]Kessen was not alone in forcefully rejecting psychology's positivist-behaviorist paradigm in which he made his early, widely-recognized contributions. Sigmund Koch serves as another compelling, still-relevant example. (See Finkelman & Kessel, 1999; Leary, 2001).

corollary, Kessen's plea for historical understanding of the child and of child development implies that gathering and analysing only quantifiable data, we will miss essential understanding of the historical and cultural embeddedness of child development. Because the complexity and the time scale of historical phenomena call for a different level of organization than that of the individual child in the here-and-now (to be studied exclusively via experimental approaches), the study of cultural historical embeddedness of human development requires different methods and analyses.

In a similar spirit: The anthropologically informed, ethnographically sophisticated developmental psychologist whose research entails making observations of and conducting conversations with children (and their families) in diverse cultures seeks to capture those in field notes that, in the best case, serve as the basis for rich, meaningful narratives about the meanings of child behavior and experience in such contexts. Such plausible stories cannot be replaced by exclusive quantitative analysis of isolated variables. This illustrates Lischoten's caution: To gain understanding of local knowledge and dynamics at the level of cultural complexity, research calls for subtle stories and not purely quantitative analyses and models based on a certain conception of the natural sciences.

The empirical-analytically minded researcher thus tries to find the most precise answer possible at the level of complexity that defines or represents the problem focus of the research. Even if that most precise answer is in the form of a verbal explanation, it is still possible and even necessary to try to test the tenability of a hypothesis by examining opposing hypotheses (as a non-numerical, verbal form of Popperian falsification).

What we are advocating is best considered 'methodological liberalism', which implies that, in adopting an *empirical-analytical* approach, the researcher seeks to collect and fit data at the level of the organization of the object of study, and that these data are analyzed as accurately as possible. If possible, and where appropriate, researchers derive and analyse data using numbers/statistics; but if this is not possible at the given level of organization, or meaningful in the context of the problem being studied, then the researcher should turn positively to narratives. As suggested above: At some levels of organisation mathematical models are not feasible or even desirable, so narrative accounts are preferable. But even then it is possible to profit from Popper's falsification ideal: The goal should always be to search systematically for a convincing, possibly conclusive argument that is *in conflict with* the conclusion. It is, for example, acceptable within modern psychology to test statistically whether a mathematical model is 'fitting'. Popper might have regretted this, for such an approach is the opposite of his falsificationism. However, even within such a 'model-fitting' research approach, respect could be paid to Popper's falsificationism by systematically exploring alternative, contrasting models.

In summary, even though – humbly echoing Kessen – we are anti-positivists, we too are not opposed to empirically-oriented developmental psychology.

Our view is that developmental psychology should be empirical-analytical in overall methodology while recognizing and accepting that empirical data cannot, indeed should not, be more exact than appropriate for the level of organization of the studied phenomenon. Among other things, this means that research methods can be qualitative or quantitative; that while data collection and analysis seek to be as exact and detailed as possible, sometimes they will – indeed should – consist of the systematic interpretation of texts and citations, other times of statistical data derived via measurements. Indeed, over the past couple of decades clear signs have emerged that qualitative methods, of various kinds, are being accepted as both legitimate and important forms of developmental inquiry (Jessor, Colby, & Shweder, 1996; Kessel, 2013; Weisner, 2005) and psychology more broadly (Bevan & Kessel, 1994; Josselson, 2017; Packer, 2004; Willig & Rogers, 2008).

4. Principles and history

In the previous sections, drawing on an admittedly shorthand review of some previous ideas from the philosophy of science that undermined positivism, we have attempted to delineate some of our 'pluralistic' methodological and epistemological convictions. As a corollary, we suggest it is *still* all too simplifying and seductive to take classical, Newtonian physics as a model for the study of human and social phenomena. Given different levels of organization (that is, different levels of complexity of phenomena studied), we need to continue to develop, adapt, and accept a variety of different methodologies, i.e., many forms of descriptive-analytic narrative approaches as well as 'conventional' experimental-statistical methods. Nor can there be a simple formula for making insightful decisions about which method is best suited to the topic, issue, and level of organization at hand. And more: A critical scientific discipline will strive to be knowledgeable about its own history and engaged in self-critical reflection on its foundations.

It is therefore of great and immediate importance that developmental psychology focuses on questions that deal with the foundations and history of the field. This is more urgent than gathering ever more 'empirical' data and adding ever more 'empirical' papers to myriad journals. It is particularly essential to establish understanding of the discipline's intellectual *and* institutional context, rather than only accumulating further fragmented and complicating, or worse, simplifying knowledge. To that end, in our view critical historical analysis is essential. As the papers in this special issue make clear, past and present (and future) empirical research on child behavior and experience is intricately connected with the history of theories and assumptions about children and their development. Moreover, self-critical knowledge of the history of the discipline itself can help prevent the reinvention of the wheel or, to adapt another metaphor, simply (and misleadingly) placing old wine in shiny new bottles. While research practice *within* the discipline requires defined empirical-analytical methodology (both qualitative and quantitative), study of the structure and nature *of* the discipline requires extended contemplation, analysis, and critical thinking, especially about its past as embedded in the present and future. (Below we address the central question of how, where, and by whom such analysis and thinking are best conducted.)

5. Concluding discussion

The fact that Kessen referred to the child as a 'cultural invention' might be taken to mean he was suggesting that children are not (also) biological beings. We should realize, however, that, via his title and related analysis, Kessen sought to provoke self-critical reflection. In effect, he wanted to wake up those he saw as mainstream and misguided 'positivistic dreamers'. The child is *also* a cultural invention, a product of the 'Zeitgeist'. Kessen challenges developmental psychologists to be critically aware of their (normative) concepts of the child, concepts which they absorb, reinforce, and reify in their own theories and methods, influenced by the socio-cultural zeitgeist, and which they are inclined to regard and present as empirically established, universal, value-free laws of nature.

Consider the example of the decisive role of early experience, an assumption often adhered to in the nineteenth century, consistent with the sentimentalized child image of that century. It is at least debatable how decisive early experiences are; but it is comforting to adhere to this view, in part because, as Kagan (1984) asserted, it dovetails with and reinforces the convictions of the wider public. He argued that developmental psychologists find it hard to consider contra-indications seriously and prefer to keep adhering to the notion of early determinism. For him, defending this absolute early determinism is as intelligent as Ptolemy 'proving' that the earth is the stable center of the universe (Kagan, 1984, p. XI). Of course, in light of many findings since 1984, early experience and education are undoubtedly important. But Kagan objected, in our view appropriately, to overgeneralizing and overvaluing early development as uniquely causal in determining life course outcomes. In essence, Kagan wanted researchers to refrain from uncritically adopting general culturally-shaped assumptions, concluding that 'We celebrate empirical science because it corrects pleasing, but not always accurate, intuitions.' (l.c., p. X).

It is important that the celebration of empirical science does not lapse into a positivistic tendency in the sense that we have described here. So, although this may be a primarily rhetorical point, why is it that it has recently become de rigueur to emphasize that we are engaged in developmental *science*? For one thing, what does that imply about the (ir)relevance of multi-dimensional disciplines such as anthropology and history for shedding light on the complexities of human development in rich and diverse socio-cultural contexts? And on the same theme: When child developmental inquiry was institutionalized (in North

America) in the 1920s. It was explicitly seen as a multi- or even inter-disciplinary endeavor. Only later (primarily in the post-World-War II era) did it come to be regarded and practiced as developmental *psychology*; moreover, one specific conception and form of the discipline, viz., 'experimental' and, in essence, positivistic (Kessel, 2009). Is there now meaningful movement away from that restrictive, uni-disciplinary perspective? Perhaps. (See our concluding comments.)

Our view of what empirical-analytical research should be seems to dovetail with what Kagan proposed when he wrote that 'The Vienna philosophers went too far in their accommodation to the new discoveries in physics . . .' (l.c., p. XIII). Consistent with what we suggested earlier about the *Wiener Kreis*, Kagan serves to illustrate that Kessen's critical, post-positivist chords are being echoed and amplified by many (developmental) psychologists. (See Bronfenbrenner, Kessel, Kessen, & White, 1986; Brown & Cole, 2001; Kessel, 1983) And that includes the authors of the papers in this issue (as we hope will be evident).

An important closing question is whether Kessen's critique and the contributions in this special issue are unduly oriented towards the West, or global North. While these papers, for practical reasons of manageability, are primarily focused on trends in Europe and the United States, we suggest that the analyses and understanding emerging from the study of the history of childhood – exemplified by the contributions here – can be generalized to other continents and regions.

Stearns' book about *Childhood in World History* (2006) is an instructive example. Because, however reluctant and careful he is in generalizing Western developments to the rest of the world, Stearns nevertheless makes it clear that contemporary globalization reflects general trends regarding the changing contexts of child and family life. In particular, the transition from agricultural to modern societies – such as first occurred after the Enlightenment in Europe and North America – offers a number of discernible general patterns. For example, children who no longer contribute to the workforce but go to school to learn what is now considered relevant for their future functioning in the community or society; also, children who have fewer siblings and will die at an early age much less frequently than previously. And while the order and causal relationships between these dynamic changes may differ at different locations in the world and at different points in time, such patterns do indeed occur worldwide.

As another example, Stearns believes that the emphasis on the striving for children's happiness has also become a global tendency which is subtly interlinked with these other patterns. Thus, the decrease of child mortality and increase in health care, as well as increased welfare, allows more room for concerns about 'happiness' (Stearns, 2010, 2011).

Thus, while the majority of the papers of this special issue are primarily focused on elements of Western culture, we should emphasize that this is not an unintended expression of a form of ethnocentrism but, rather, because historical trends in the West are also unfolding in other parts of the world as a function of modernization processes (Koops & de Winter, 2011). Moreover, as powerfully illustrated by the Keller and Vicedo papers in this issue, a reciprocal process is underway, where both historical and culturally-informed scholarship prompt a critical perspective on core, deeply-entrenched mainstream assumptions and theories. In their case, the focus is on attachment theory and research; a parallel process is now underway regarding the presumed 'word gap', i.e., supposed consequential deficiencies in the verbal environments of poor children, including those in contexts outside the North America and Europe, compared to their more affluent peers. (See Avineri & Johnson, 2015; Miller & Sperry, 2012)

The articles collected in this special issue will, we hope, encourage further (self-)critical historical research, further contributions to what might be called Historical Developmental Psychology (Koops & Elder, 1996). That, in turn, reflects two related and fundamental features of what a generative post-positivist paradigm entails: First, affirmative recognition that (developmental) psychology is, at root, a 'moral science' (White, 1983a), where normative assumptions are embedded, more or less explicitly, in both theory and practice, and most fundamentally in the very notion(s) of 'development' itself (White, 1983b). And second:

> An historical [developmental] psychology involves, … in the first place, an awareness of the historicity of the very norms that are dominant in a given culture or within a given science at a given time. In the second place, an historical [developmental] psychology takes seriously the variety of culturally and socially operative factors that go into the very constitution of such norms, whether of childhood, or of cognitive development [or of social development], and at the same time an historical [developmental] psychology is aware or critically self-aware of the status of its own operative norms and methods of inquiry … An historical [developmental] psychology is thus, necessarily, a normative psychology, not only in the descriptive sense of studying prevalent or historical norms, but also in the *critical* sense of rejecting and proposing norms. (Wartofsky, 1983, p. 189; see also, Bronfenbrenner et al., 1986, p. 1227)

And this follow-up passage powerfully underlines our overall theme (on the critical role of historical developmental psychology, and psychologists):

> [None of this means] we can't get started until we all agree on the norms. But it puts the determination and critique of norms right in the ballpark as a concern of actual psychological theory and psycho logical practice. [This] doesn't mean every psychologist has to do so every day or say it as a little prayer every morning. But it means that it [the determination and critique of norms becomes an integral part of the field … and not some after-hours, cracker-barrel stuff you do when the real psychologists aren't around … which is its usual status. That is, consideration of norms has to become integral to the field such that those who are doing it are in touch with those who aren't, making them aware of it and so percolating the field. (op cit., p. 219)

All of which, we believe, both reinforces and honors Bill Kessen's plea for a cultural-historical approach to the study of child and human development (Kessel, 1991).

6. Brief overview of the papers in this issue

We are pleased to record that this special issue originated in Ann Arbor, Michigan on 12–14 May 2016 in a symposium on 'Historical Perspectives on Child Development: Implications for Future Research' organized by then-still-in-place History Committee of the Society for Research in Child Development (SRCD). In essence the following papers are the written, final versions of the symposium presentations by members of the Committee and other guests. Appreciative of the Society's support for that event, we conclude this introduction with the following Socratically-intended comments.

At least in its current stated strategic goals (Sherrod, 2016), SRCD – perhaps the most influential organization of its kind – is signaling commitments to some of the suggestions we have made here. As a noteworthy example, it has declared the goal of returning to its, and the field's, multi/inter-disciplinary roots. Similarly, there is announced emphasis on seeking understanding of the cultural and contextual dimensions of human development, with a presumed greater receptivity to qualitative forms of inquiry still more widely practiced in disciplines such as cultural and linguistic anthropology and history; also, a recent, loosely-related focus on 'social justice'. And there are some signs of a recognition that relationships, both institutional and intellectual, between the global north and south need to become more reciprocal, where theories, methods and findings are open to critique and fundamental revision from outside–the-mainstream perspectives. (See, e.g., Dawes, 2016; Kessel & Lukowski, 2016; Verma, 2016)

How will these commitments be institutionally enacted, most notably in the planning and review processes for both SRCD's highly sought-after biennial meetings and its visible, high-impact journals? For a range of reasons, including the understandable inertial dynamics of large professional-scientific organizations, our view is that only time will tell how deep and consequential such projected philosophical and substantive shifts will be.

In particular, and again for a combination of reasons, we are skeptical – though hopeful – that the Society and the field as a widespread whole will create significant space for the kind of critical historical-developmental scholarship that these papers so persuasively represent. Such space would signal recognition, for example, that twenty-first Century 'history' is far from being a single, stand-alone 'discipline' but, instead, variously engages issues at the intersection of culture, society, politics and both epistemology and moral philosophy.

So will we get to the stage when, in Wartofsky's perennially challenging words, '[the determination and critique] of norms [are] integral to the field such that those who are doing it are in touch with those who aren't, making them aware of it and so percolating the field'? Seeing such self-critical engagement with normative and moral (and political) questions as akin to a final post-positivist frontier for developmental inquiry (at least in our professional lifetimes), and inspired by these papers, we will strive to keep hope alive!

Consistent with the main theme of this collection, Steven Mintz (*Why history matters: Placing infant and child development in historical perspective*) underscores the importance of systematic knowledge about how conceptions of childhood vary across social time and space. In the process, he demonstrates how such understanding helps rebut myths, undercuts linear views of progress (and thus 'development'), and sheds light on often misunderstood long-term trends and processes.

With a focus on changing social views and standards regarding children and emotions, Peter Stearns (*Children and emotions history*) provides a detailed case study of the overall themes underlined by Mintz. He examines, in socio-cultural context, two major changes in American approaches (around 1800 and in the 1920s), as well as possible explanations for shifts in specific emotions (e.g., happiness and shame). In a more 'meta' mode, he considers complexities in discussing changes or continuities in children's emotions, *and* reflects on the possibilities for connections between historical and psychological approaches.

As a complement to Stearns' paper, Paul Harris (*Emotion, imagination and the world's furniture*) considers how a particular conception of emotions that emerged in the late nineteenth century was uncritically embedded in the work of subsequent generations of psychologists (at least in Europe and North America). Highlighting that conception's heavily evolutionary-biological underpinnings, he then examines two species-specific qualities of human emotions, where culture and imagination are central. Finally, he suggests that such a framework would be generative in considering connections between the history of emotions and their development in children.

Focusing on how John Bowlby's and Mary Ainsworth's ethological theory of attachment was received in different disciplinary communities, Marga Vicedo (*Putting attachment in its place: Disciplinary and cultural contexts*) makes two essential points: From Margaret Mead's 1950s anthropological-critique onwards, cultural challenges to the theory's central assumptions (e.g., of universality) have been essentially ignored. And second, that such a (dys)functional dynamic can be best explained in terms of different disciplinary paradigms – philosophical and methodological, positivist and not. She thus provides an insightful illustration of some of the themes presented above, not least how fine-grained historical-archival research can shed illuminating light on major areas of 'mainstream developmental science'.

Heidi Keller (*Cultural and historical diversity in early relationship formation*) complements both Vicedo's paper and, again, parts of the 'post-positivist' view presented above. Drawing on the work of cultural psychologists and anthropologists, as well as context-attuned developmental psychologists (herself included), she reviews how caregiving/socialization beliefs and patterns vary, consequentially, across changing sociocultural environments and historical time. She concludes with reflections on how the often-assumed contradiction between cultural-historical specificity and universality, e.g., in the realm of attachment and overall early relationship formation, can be overcome. As a corollary, she too illustrates how historical and developmental analysis can and should be two sides of the same analytic coin.

Lassonde's focus (*Authority, disciplinary intimacy & parenting in middle-class America*) is on historical shifts, from the mid-19th-century through to the present, in beliefs and childcare advice regarding appropriate styles of parenting. Examining such topics as views regarding corporal punishment and its presumed link to authoritarianism, his analysis emphasizes the importance of understanding changing dynamics in wider socio-cultural-political contexts, not least for critically locating the contingent views of developmental 'experts' (during various periods). And although the patterns he discerns are based in the United States, that sort of analytic principle and goal is no less important for work elsewhere, i.e., historical-developmental research (on 'parenting') that can yield a picture of differences and similarities across time and space(s).

As a broad complement to Lassonde's paper, Sandin (*The parent: A cultural invention. The politics of parenting*) explores how – in Sweden in the twentieth century – beliefs, practices, and policies regarding the relative roles of parents and social institutions in fostering and protecting children were significantly shaped by the philosophy of the wider welfare state. He analyzes how government policies and (interventionist) practices both reflected and reified assumptions, for example, about limited parental responsibility, especially in relation to children seen as competent, individual agents with adult-like rights; such assumptions were, in turn, tied to certain notions of 'developmental well-being' and reinforced by certain international conventions.

In the end, then, the harmonious sounding of some distinctly Bill Kessen-like themes!

Disclosure statement

No potential conflict of interest was reported by the authors.

References

Adorno, T. W., Albert, H., & Dahrendorf, R. (1993). *Der Positivismusstreit in der deutschen Soziologie*. München: DTV.

Avineri, N., & Johnson, E. (2015). Introduction to "Bridging the Word Gap". *Linguistic Anthropology, 25*, 67–68.

Bevan, W., & Kessel, F. S. (1994). Plain truths and home cooking: Notes on the making and remaking of psychology. *American Psychologist, 49*, 505–509.

Blumenthal, A. L. (1977). Wilhelm Wundt and early American psychology" A clash of two cultures. *Annals of the New York Academy of Sciences, 291*, 13–20.

Boring, E. G. (1950). *A history of experimental psychology*. New York, NY: Appleton.

Bourdeau, M. (2011). Auguste comte. In E. N. Zalta (Ed.), *The Stanford encyclopedia of philosophy*. Stanford: Stanford University.

Bronfenbrenner, U., Kessel, F., Kessen, W., & White, S. (1986). Toward a critical social history of developmental psychology: A propaedeutic discussion. *American Psychologist, 41*, 1218–1230.

Brown, K., & Cole, M. (2001). A Utopian methodology as a tool for cultural and critical psychologies: Toward a positive critical theory. In M. J. Packer, & M. B. Tappan (Eds.), *Cultural and critical perspectives on human development* (pp. 41–66). New York, NY: SUNY Press.

Busato, V. (2014). A.D. de Groot(1914-2006): Meester in de psychologie. In V. Busato, M. van Essen, & W. Koops (Red.), *Van fenomenologie naar empirisch analytische psychologie* (249–314). Amsterdam: Bert Bakker.

Cole, M. (1996). *Cultural psychology: A once and future discipline*. Cambridge: Harvard University Press.

Comte, A. (1844). *Discours sur l'esprit positif*. Paris: Pain et Thunot.

Dahms, H.-J. (1994). *Positivismusstreit. Die Auseinandersetzungen der Frankfurter Schule mit dem logischen Positivismus, dem amerikanischen Pragmatismus und dem Kritíschen Rationalismus*. Frankfurt am Main: Suhrkamp.

Danziger, K. (1979). The positivist repudiation of Wundt. *Journal of the History of the Behavioral Sciences, 15*, 205–230.

Dawes, A. (2016). The interface of rights and knowledge? *Developments (SRCD Newsletter)., 59*, 4–5.

Delanty, G., & Strydom, P. (2003). *Philosophies of social science: The classic and contemporary readings*. London: Open University.

Finkelman, D., & Kessel, F. S. (Eds.). (1999). *Sigmund Koch: Psychology in human context – Essays in dissidence and reconstruction*. Chicago, IL: The University of Chicago Press.

Goodnow, J., Miller, P., & Kessel, F. S. (Eds.). (1995). *Cultural practices as contexts for development. New directions in child development, No. 67*. San Francisco, CA: Jossey Bass.

de Groot, A. D. (1961). *Methodologie. Grondslagen van onderoek en denken in de gedragswetenschappen*. Amsterdam: Noordhollandse Uitgeversmaatschappij.

de Groot, A. D. (1969). *Methodology. Foundations of inference and research in the behavioral sciences*. Den Haag: Mouton.

Jessor, R., Colby, A., & Shweder, R. A. (Eds.). (1996). *Ethnography and human development: Context and meaning in social inquiry*. Chicago, IL: The University of Chicago Press.

Josselson, R. (2017). Editorial. *Qualitative Psychology, 4*(1), 1.

Kagan, J. (1984). *The nature of the child*. New York, NY: Basic Books.

Kessel, F. S. (1969). The philosophy of science as proclaimed and science as practiced: "Identity" or "dualism"? *American Psychologist, 24*, 999–1005.

Kessel, F. S. (1983). On cultural construction and reconstruction in psychology: Voices in conversation. In F. S. Kessel & A. W. Siegel (Eds.), *The child and other cultural inventions*. New York, NY: Praeger.

Kessel, F. S. (1991). Vision, scholarship, and the child. In F. S. Kessel, M. H. Bornstein, & A. J. Sameroff (Eds.), *Contemporary constructions of the child: Essays in honor of William Kessen*. Hillsdale, NJ: Erlbaum.

Kessel, F. S. (2009). Research on child development: Historical perspectives. In R. A. Shweder, et al. (Eds.), *The child: An encyclopedic companion*. Chicago, IL: The University of Chicago Press.

Kessel, F. S. (2013). On the qualities, and quality, of qualitative (developmental) research: Some semi-random reflections. *ISSBD Bulletin*, Serial No., *64*, 6–8.

Kessel, F. S., & Lukowski, A. (2016). Global perspectives. *Developments (SRCD Newsletter)., 59*(1), 1.

Kessel, F. S., & Siegel, A. W. (Eds.). (1983). *The child and other cultural inventions*. New York, NY: Praeger.

Kessen, W. (1965). *The child*. New York, NY: Wiley.

Kessen, W. (1979). The American child and other cultural inventions. *American Psychologist, 34*, 815–820.

Kessen, W. (1983). The child and other cultural inventions. In F. S. Kessel, & A. W. Siegel (Eds.), *The child and other cultural inventions* (pp. 26–39). New York, NY: Praeger.

Koops, W. (2016). *Een beeld van een kind*. Amsterdam: Boom (Images of children).

Koops, W., & de Winter, M. (Red.). (2011). *Wereldwijd opvoeden* (Global education). Amsterdam: SWP.

Koops, W., & Elder, G. H., Jr. (1996). Historical developmental psychology: some introductory remarks. *International Journal of Behavioral Development, 19*, 369–371.

Leary, D. E. (1979). Wundt and after: Psychology's shifting relations with the natural sciences, social sciences, and philosophy. *Journal of the History of the Behavioral Sciences, 15*, 231–241.

Leary, D. E. (2001). One big idea, one ultimate concern: Sigmund Koch's critique of psychology and hope for the future. *American Psychologist, 56*, 425–432.

Linschoten, J. (1964). *Idolen van de psycholoog* (Idols of Psychologists). Utrecht: Bijleveld.

Miller, P. J., & Sperry, D. E. (2012). Déjà vu: The continuing misrecognition of low-income children's verbal abilities. In H. R. Markus, & S. Fiske (Eds.), *Facing social class: How societal rank influences interaction*. New York, NY: Russell Sage Foundation.

Packer, M. (2004). Editorial. *Qualitative Research in Psychology, 1*, 265.

Popper, K. (1935). *Logik der Forschung*. Wenen: Julius Springer Verlag.

Popper, K. (1959). *The logic of scientific discovery*. London: Hutchinson.

Popper, K. (1963). *Conjectures and refutations: The growth of scientific knowledge*. London: Routledge.

Rogoff, B. (2003). *The cultural. Nature of human development*. New York, NY: Oxford University Press.

Sherrod, L. (2016). SRCD in the 21st century. *Developments (SRCD Newsletter)., 59*(3), 1–2.

Shweder, R. A. (1994). *Thinking through cultures: Expeditions in cultural psychology*. Cambridge: Harvard University Press.

Stassijns, K., & van Strijten, J. (Red.). (2004). *De mooiste van William Wordsworth* [The most beautiful poems of William Wordsworth]. Amsterdam: Lannoo en Atlas.

Stearns, P. N. (2006). *Childhood in world history*. New York, NY: Routledge.

Stearns, P. N. (2010). Defining happy childhoods: Assessing a recent change. *The Journal of the History of Childhood and Youth, 3*, 165–186.

Steel, C. (1989). *Historische inleiding tot de Wijsbegeerte* [Historical introduction to Philosophy]. Leuven: Universitaire Pers Leuven.

Verma, S. (2016). A coalition with a truly international agenda. *Developments (SRCD Newsletter)., 59*, 2–3.

Wartofsky, M. (1983). The child's construction of the world and the world's construction of the child: From historical epistemology to historical psychology. In F. S. Kessel, & A. W. Siegel (Eds.). (1983). *The child and other cultural inventions*. New York, NY: Praeger.

Weisner, T. S. (Ed.). (2005). *Discovering successful pathways in children's development: Mixed methods in the study of childhood and family life*. Chicago, IL: The University of Chicago Press.

White, S. H. (1983a). Psychology as a moral science. In F. S. Kessel, & A. W. Siegel (Eds.), *The child and other cultural inventions*. New York, NY: Praeger.

White, S. H. (1983b). The idea of development in developmental psychology. In R. M. Lerner (Ed.), *Developmental psychology: Historical and philosophical perspectives*. Hillsdale, NJ: Erlbaum.

Willig, C., & Rogers, W. S. (2008). *Handbook of qualitative methods in psychology*. Thousand Oaks, CA: Sage.

Wundt, W. M. (1900-1920). *Völkerpsychologie. Bnd. 1-2: Die Sprache(1900); Bnd 3: Die Kunst (1908); Bnd. 4-5-6: Mythos und Religion (1910-1914); Bnd. 7-8: Die Gesellschaft (1917); Bnd. 9: Das Recht (1918); Bnd. 10: Kultur in der Geschichte (1920)*. Leipzig: Engelmann.

Why history matters: Placing infant and child development in historical perspective

Steven Mintz

ABSTRACT
How knowledge of the history of childhood problematizes many common assumptions about child development, rebuts myths that distort public understanding, refutes simplistic linear theories of progress and reveals certain long-term trends, developments and processes that are otherwise misunderstood.

Why is knowledge of history valuable to those who study infant and child development? At first glance, history seems irrelevant to the kinds of empirical and applied research questions that contribute to a scientific understanding of infancy and childhood. The topics that preoccupy developmental psychologists – such as infant and child psychology, children's cognitive, social, and emotional development, developmental disabilities, and emotional and behavioral disorders – seem profoundly ahistorical. The methods deployed by developmentalists – controlled laboratory experiments, psychometric testing, sociometric monitoring, long-term observation, and ethnographic description – differ radically from the kinds of archival research, textual analysis, and exploration of context characteristic of history as a discipline. History's only value, it would appear, is as a source of engaging anecdotes, a litany of examples of past ignorance, or a laboratory to test contemporary theories. Yet in diverse ways, a knowledge of history is essential to a scientific understanding of human development.

The historical examples I will cite come primarily from the history of the United States. But I will look at the American experience through a wide-angled lens, placing developments in the United States in comparative, cross-cultural perspective.

How, then, might history be of value to developmentalists? First, because history defamiliarizes the present, reminding us that concepts, practices, and assumptions that we take for granted are in fact problematic and time-bound. Take the Freudian notion that early childhood determines a child's future development, shapes their personality, and leaves a lasting imprint on their future relationships. Few thinkers would have accepted these ideas prior to the twentieth century. Thus in his 1749 novel *The History of Tom Jones, a Foundling*, Henry Fielding dismissed the title character's childhood in six words: 'nothing happened worthy of being recorded.'

Or take the assumption that young children are incapable of performing sophisticated chores. In most past societies, children assumed work responsibilities as young as two or three (Lancy, 2011). Abraham Lincoln, for example, assisted his father in clearing fields when the future president was only two years old. Or take the view popularized by attachment theorists that proper child development requires secure attachment to a single mothering figure and a stable household environment. In fact, most children in the past had multiple nurturing figures and shifted frequently among households (Hrdy, 2009). Or, more controversially, consider current medical advice that co-sleeping arrangements, where a mother and her infant share the same bed, put children at risk. In the past, it was highly unusual for mothers and infants to sleep apart, and even in the United States, reliance on cribs for nighttime sleeping dates only to the early twentieth century. Separate sleeping arrangements for infants reflect U.S. society's increasing emphasis on cultivating individualism from a very early age (Davies, 1995).

Then, too, history rebuts myths that distort public understanding. Take the myth of the carefree childhood. Many cling to a fantasy that childhood in the past was a time of carefree adventure; for most earlier children, however, growing up was anything but easy. Disease, family disruption, and early entry into the world of work were integral parts of childhood well into the early twentieth century irrespective of social class. The notion of a prolonged childhood, devoted to education and free from adult-like responsibilities, is a very recent invention, a product of the past century and a half, and one that only became a reality for a majority of children in the United States and Western Europe after World War II (Mintz, 2004).

Another myth is the home as a bastion of stability in an ever-changing world. Throughout U.S. history, family stability has been the exception, not the norm. At the beginning of the twentieth century, fully a third of all American children spent at least a portion of their childhood in a single-parent home, and as recently as 1940, one child in ten did not live with either parent, compared to one in 25 today (Gordon & McLanahan, 1991).

A third myth is that childhood is a status transcending class, ethnicity, and gender. In fact, every aspect of childhood is shaped by class, ethnicity, gender, geography, religion, and historical era. Not simply a biological phenomenon, childhood is better understood as a life stage whose contours are shaped by a particular time, place, and cultural context. Childrearing practices, schooling, and the age at which young people leave home – all are products of particular social and cultural circumstances. Even the age of sexual maturation appears to vary on the basis of context (Schultz, 1995).

A fourth myth is that the United States is a peculiarly child-friendly society. In actuality, Americans are deeply ambivalent about children. Adults envy young people their youth, vitality, and physical attractiveness, but also resent children's intrusions on their time and frequently fear their passions. Over time, the United States has become an increasingly age segregated society, in which children's contacts with adults other than parents are confined to specialists: teachers, pediatricians, child psychologists, music or dance instructors, and coaches. Many reforms nominally designed to protect the young were instituted to insulate adults from children and insure smooth operation of the economic order (Chudacoff, 1989).

Lastly a myth, perhaps the most difficult to overcome, is a myth of progress or its inverse, of decline. Often, the history of childhood becomes a story of steps forward over time: of parental engagement replacing emotional distance, leniency supplanting strict punishment, and scientific enlightenment superseding superstition and misguided moralism. This viewpoint is sometimes seen in reverse: that children are losing their innocence and playfulness too quickly, that overzealous parents are undercutting their offsprings' independence by coddling and indulging their kids. Both the Whiggish myth of progress and the declensionist myth of decline are highly misleading. Historical change invariably involves trade-offs. Children benefited from dramatic declines in rates of infant and child mortality and increased control over childhood diseases. But the young have fewer ways to demonstrate their growing competence and maturity (apart from sports) and more children than ever suffer from disabilities and chronic conditions (Golden, Meckel, Richard, & Prescott, 2004).

History refutes simplistic linear theories of progress and crude assumptions about inevitability. One striking example involves child abuse. Although the physical and sexual abuse of children has declined in recent years, other forms of abuse remain prevalent, as the literary critic Daniel Kline has observed. These include the violence of expectations – the assumption that children are able to achieve certain markers of maturity before previous eras deemed them physiologically or psychologically ready; the violence of labeling – of attaching pathological labels upon normal childish behavior; the violence of representation – the sexual exploitation of images of girls in advertising; and the violence of poverty, which exposes children to extraordinary stresses and limits their future possibilities (Kline, 1998).

In addition, history reveals certain long-term trends, developments, and processes that we are otherwise blind to. Examples include the long-term shift from an environment in which children were supposed to respect and obey their parents to one where parents seek to earn their children's love; or the triumph of therapeutic discourse, which uses psychological categories to understand children's behavior. History also offers valuable lessons: That even young children are more capable than contemporary societies assume or that ideas about children's nature and how best to rear kids have always been contested (Hulbert, 2003).

Equally important, history allows us to view present-day controversies from a novel vantage point and offers dynamic, diachronic, longitudinal perspectives different from those generally advanced by psychology or sociology. By treating concepts and behavior as constructs, history underscores the radical contingency of all social arrangements and modes of thought. In addition to stressing the importance of change over time, history also emphasizes the significance of social and cultural context in shaping the nature and timing of key life course developments, such as leaving the parental home, attending school, or entering the workforce. History reminds us that conceptions of childhood and children's essential nature, theories of child development, and approaches to childrearing have shifted profoundly over time. With its emphasis on four C's – change over time, the significance of context, the role of contingency in shaping historical development, and the ever-present reality of conflict and contestation – history greatly enriches and challenges insights gleaned from the other social sciences.

What is childhood?

Nothing better illustrates the value of history than asking: What is childhood? Is childhood an age range, a period of physical and emotional immaturity, a phase of physiological and psychological development, a label, or a socially-constructed category that varies according to class and cultural context? The answer, of course, is all of the above.

Childhood is a stage of life whose boundaries and cultural meaning vary markedly over time. In seventeenth-century Europe, childhood, by recent standards, began late and ended early. It followed infancy, which referred to the phase of life in which a young person was under a mother's control, and did not end until around the age of five or six. Childhood was succeeded by youth, which began around ten or twelve and extended into the early or even late twenties (Chudacoff, 1989).

Childhood is also a developmental phase, but one whose attributes have been defined in very different ways. At various times, children have been regarded as animal-like, innately sinful, pure and innocent, cute and playful, and, recently, incipient scientists. In addition, childhood needs to be understood in terms of institutional arrangements and social roles that have varied widely. In the twentieth century, childhood became synonymous with school attendance. In the past, in contrast, many children spent substantial amounts of time as servants or wards in other families' residences.

Childhood is anything but a marginal subject. The history of childhood is bound up with key cultural, economic, historical, psychological, and sociological themes. These range from the structural – such as the growth of the state's police and administrative powers, the rise of modern bureaucratic institutions, the development of the welfare state, and the emergence of modern criminal jurisprudence – to the developmental, including shifting patterns of socialization, enculturation, and maturation, the cultural, such as the triumph of the therapeutic, and the economic, like the growth of a consumer economy. It is through childhood that we can see how ethnic, gender, racial, and religious identities are transmitted, and how social class makes itself felt in private life. The history of childhood also encourages us to rethink what we mean by agency, identity formation, generational consciousness, and subcultures and their relationship with mainstream culture. Childhood is the missing link between the psychological and social, the domestic and the public, the past and the future.

The history of childhood is commonly viewed from perspectives with deep historical roots. There is the Rousseauian view of child development as the story of the loss of organic wholeness, innocence, and a sense of wonder, a view that contrasts radically with that associated with the classic *bildungsroman* or coming of age story, of maturation as a form of liberation from paternal authority, familial hierarchy, and *naïveté*. Then there is the declensionist view of children growing ever more insolent, impolite, and ill-mannered, which stands at odds with a Whiggish view that emphasizes progress, defined in terms of improvements in children's health, the decline of child labor, the gradual breakdown of rigid gender roles, and increasing access to school.

Since the 1970s, as birthrates fell, increasing proportions of adults declined to bear children, and growing numbers of seniors began to live in adult-only communities, the United States became a more adult-centric society. One consequence was a hardening of attitudes toward children apparent in mass culture. Landmark depictions of children in Hollywood films – such as *Carrie*, *Taxi Driver*, or *Thirteen* – portrayed children possessed by evil spirits or employed as prostitutes or engaged in casual sex and drug use. Negative views of children could also be found in popular discourse in the United States, in the oft-repeated claim that contemporary children are coddled rather than challenged, indulged rather than pushed toward achievement. Yet at the same time, child protection represents the ultimate trump card in political and judicial discourse. Children's health care, child pornography, undocumented children, and the juvenile death penalty and life imprisonment are treated very differently than similar matters involving adults. A fundamental tension prevails, between an earlier ideal of a protected child, sheltered from the stresses and harsh realities of adult life, and the prepared child, exposed from an early age to knowledge about the adult world, the better to be able to cope with the complexities and disruptions that characterize contemporary society. Parents, as well as U.S. society as a whole, vacillate between the contradictory ideals of sheltering and shielding children from premature exposure to adult realities and preparing them to compete in a volatile, uncertain, complex, and competitive environment (Calvert, 1992).

Childrearing

The United States is unique in its preoccupation with the proper way to raise children. Americans write and read more childrearing books than those in other nations and worry more incessantly about children's well-being. As a result, it is impossible for American parents to rear children intuitively or un-self-consciously. Parents face a barrage of contradictory advice: to bottle-feed or breast feed, to co-sleep or use a crib, to use a stroller or a sling. Disagreements among childrearing experts are nothing new. Every era has been buffeted with clashing counsel, pitting those who emphasize parental authority and discipline against those who advocate affection and bonding. Since the late nineteenth century, every generation has had experts advocating a parenting style they claim is buttressed by science, only to be challenged by other authorities claiming scientific validation for their approach (Hulbert, 2003; LeVine & LeVine, 2016).

The 1920s illustrates conflicts among childrearing experts particularly vividly. Behaviorists, like the psychologist John B. Watson, advised mothers to avoid hugging, kissing, or playing with their infants and to rigidly schedule feeding and sleeping, lest their children fail to develop a capacity for self-control. Child development specialists, led by Arnold Gesell, tied certain traits to children's age and stage of development. At the same time, early Freudians anticipated Dr. Benjamin Spock by calling for a more loving relationship between mother and infants, but also worried intensely about the dangers of maternal over-involvement. What linked these contrasting viewpoints was a fear that any dysfunction in mother–child relationships would lead to lifelong psychological maladjustments.

The late nineteenth century marked the birth of a scientific approach to childrearing advice. Supplanting earlier childrearing tracts, written by ministers and moralists, were works by physicians and psychologists. Deeply concerned about high rates of infant and child mortality, authors such as Dr. L. Emmett Holt provided mothers with expert advice about hygiene. Holt, the Dr. Spock of his age, called upon mothers to adopt a regimented approach to childrearing, and to impose strict sleeping and feeding schedules (Hardyment, 2007).

Why did parents increasingly seek 'scientific' advice? Various societal changes greatly intensified parents' anxiety about their children's economic future, values, and physical and psychological well-being. First, as the American economy developed, parents found it harder to transmit their class position directly to their children. Children's future success appeared to hinge on instilling the proper values and character traits in their offspring. During the first half of the twentieth century, parents viewed toys as a way to cultivate 'proper' gender roles, with dolls cultivating maternal qualities in girls and construction toys essential for instructing boys in design and planning. Household chores, in exchange for an allowance, were a mechanism to ensure that children could delay gratification and appreciate the value of money. Boys' sports was viewed as an ideal vehicle for instilling self-discipline, channeling aggressiveness, and cultivating a capacity for team work (Chudacoff, 2007; Cross, 1999).

Second, as young people's schooling and leisure time expanded and commercial amusements proliferated, parents faced new challenges in monitoring their children's school performance, supervising and regulating their behavior outside the home, and overseeing their relations with peers. Experts offered advice to parents about how best to deal with these novel challenges. Third, the growth of psychological expertise led parents to worry about aspects of life that elicited little concern in the past, such as children's posture, sleep habits, siblings bonds, and psychological well-being. In our own time, anxiety has swirled around children's allergies, attention deficit disorder, autism, and Sudden Infant Death Syndrome – perils to which earlier generations were blind.

During the 1920s, the tenets of scientific childrearing, still upheld by authorities like John B. Watson, came under attack by advocates of new familial ideal: the 'companionate' family. According to this ideal, 'moms' and 'dads' (new words during the decade) were to be their children's big pals. The new economy of the 1920s was thought to demand a new kind of personality – less reserved and restrained and more outgoing – best nurtured in a loving family environment. The 1930s saw the psychologizing of motherhood. Freudian psychoanalysis said that early childhood was critical for child development and that even the smallest mistake in mothering carried devastating consequences. When tens of thousands of potential soldiers were deemed unfit for military service in World War II, expert opinion attacked 'Momism' – the supposedly damaging effects of smother love and over-solicitous mothering – and its polar opposite, maternal neglect. Following the war, Dr. Benjamin Spock popularized a Freudian approach to childrearing which rejected strict scheduling and advised mothers to trust themselves. But despite his association with 'permissiveness' in childrearing, Spock insisted on the importance of mothers and fathers setting and enforcing clear boundaries on children's behavior (Maier, 1998).

It is not surprising that as the composition of families frequently shifted as parents partnered and re-partnered, attachment parenting became popular. This approach not only promised to give children a strong sense of stability and connection, it was also said to contribute to children's self-esteem that would provide the resilience that needed in an insecure, ever-changeable environment. The growing popularity of attachment parenting also reflected a fundamental shift in parent–child relations. No longer did parents expect their child's love; they felt they had to earn that love.

As economic growth slowed and family incomes stagnated, childrearing advice focused on ways to foster children who would be successful in a highly competitive society. The early twenty-first century marked the rise of intensive parenting – including the highly involved soccer mom, the hovering helicopter parent, and the hyper-ambitious Tiger Mom – prompting a reaction among those who called for more relaxed form of 'free-range' parenting, which claimed to produce more creative and imaginative children.

If any lesson can be drawn from this contentious history, it is that childrearing advice is never simply about the best ways to promote children's health, happiness, or psychological well-being. It invariably reflects their parents' fears and their sense of the kind of future that their children need to be prepared for.

Shifts in parent–child relations

In recent years, the relationship between parents and children has undergone profound changes. For one thing, the decision about whether or not to have children is increasingly voluntary. Electing not to have children is no longer stigmatized as it once was, and 'child-free' adults are no longer casually dismissed as shallow and self-absorbed. As a result, the decision to have a child is increasingly deliberate and purposeful. Having a child represents a self-conscious choice to become a mother or father and to assume the responsibilities that parenting entails.

Parenting also became increasingly problematic. Lacking the clear and authoritative guidelines set by earlier childrearing experts like Dr. Benjamin Spock, moms and dads had to decide whether to be strict or lenient, achievement and performance focused, or indulgent, pushy or laid back. Today's parents receive sharply conflicting messages about whether or not to prioritize academics and other accomplishments or, instead, give their children free time, freedom, and free range to explore their environment.

At the same time, parents grew far more sensitive to the risks that their children face, both physical and psychological. Anxiety has become a hallmark of contemporary parenting. Even before their child is born, prenatal testing leads parents to worry about potential birth defects to an extent absent in the past. This is followed by a preoccupation with children's safety and their personality development, psychological well-being and academic performance. Stoking parental fears are sensationalistic media accounts of the risks posed by pedophiles and the prevalence of stranger abduction of children, as well as reports about the potential perils posed by bullying, vaccines, additives, and various environmental hazards. The 'discovery of risk' carried profound consequences for children's upbringing. Parents kept their kids under closer supervision, kept them indoors much more than in the past, and narrowed the geography in which children were allowed to roam (Furedi, 2001; Rothschild, 2005; Stearns, 2003).

These years also witnessed the politicization of childrearing advice with bitter disputes about breastfeeding, pacifiers, spanking, co-sleeping, and vaccination. Partisan and religious divides emerged in attitudes toward forms of discipline and structure within families, with social conservatives tending to favor greater emphasis on parental authority and liberals preferring time-outs and reasoning with children to any form of physical punishment.

As mothers and fathers devoted more time to work, a sense of guilt also colored parent–child relations. Even though parents actually spend more face-to-face time with their children than did their 1950s counterparts, mothers and fathers worried that they are not able to provide the kind of safe, secure, stable childhood they themselves enjoyed, involving a great deal of free unstructured play with neighborhood friends. Consequently, many overcompensate.

Underlying these changes in parent–child relationships are a raft of historic shifts. Delayed parenthood, better educated parents, and reduced birthrates led parents to increase their fixation upon individual children. In a society in which marital relationships had grown much more fragile, many parents looked to their children as a source of permanent attachment and emotional fulfillment. The increase in single parenthood and two-earner households also altered parent–child relations, since children in these settings must take on greater responsibility for self-care and helping out than did those in homes with full-time, stay-at-home mothers.

Perhaps the biggest force for change in parent–child relationships lies in parents' worries about their ability to transmit their class status to their children. As the economy has grown more competitive and entrepreneurial, many parents seek to give their child a leg up, and as a result invest more time and resources in enrichment activities: reading to their children, conversing with them, and providing toys and activities aimed at enhancing their development. Nor does parenting end at 18 or 21. Most parents not only expect to contribute to their children's college education, but to its aftermath: To supporting them during their twenties and helping them, later, in making a down payment on a house.

For all the disdainful talk about hovering, over involved, and overprotective helicopter parents, the fact is that parents today are, on average, closer to their adult children than in the past. parent–child hierarchy has given way, to a remarkable extent, to relationships that are closer, more intimate, and more egalitarian than existed in the past. If it has become harder for some children to cut the umbilical cord and establish an independent identity, and if it has become more difficult for some parents to let go and grant their kids a fully autonomous life, for many children and parents alike, the ongoing bond between child and parent proves to be a crucial source of meaning and personal happiness.

Contemporary childhood in historical perspective

American childhood today differs radically from childhood just a generation ago. Children are more diverse ethnically and more are born outside of marriage. Significantly fewer live with their biological father or a step-father. More are only children and more have stepsiblings. Children's lived experience has changed in other ways as well. Kids spend more time in front of screens of various sorts, and children's play, especially for the upper middle class, is more likely to be electronic or adult organized and supervised. As a result of a sharp upsurge in maternal employment, kids experience sharper swings between periods of freedom and intense parental involvement, and more time in structured situations, from play dates to organized sports and various enrichment activities. Meanwhile, parental guilt has contributed to an expectation that children should be happy and never bored. One manifestation of this development is that parents spend far more money on individual children than in the past on toys and entertainment. There is, however, a deepening class divide in parental investments in and expenditures upon children.

Despite widespread public anxieties, far-reaching transformations in childhood have not adversely affected children's well-being. By most measures, kids today are doing better than their predecessors a generation ago. Children's death rates have fallen, fewer smoke, and test scores have risen. More graduate from high school and enroll in college. Still, profound concerns persist, and these are related primarily to continuing inequities in the experience of childhood rooted in class, race, ethnicity, and gender.

The history of western childhood from the early nineteenth century through the mid-twentieth century involved recurrent attempts to universalize a middle-class conception of childhood. According to this ideal, children were vulnerable, malleable beings who needed to be kept at home or school into their teens and insulated from the contaminating influence of adult realities. This view represented a sharp contrast with the past, when children moved frequently between the natal home and residence elsewhere, and early entry into work responsibilities was virtually universal. Especially striking is an apparent lack of concern for children's welfare. In colonial America, infants and children frequently suffered severe burns playing near fireplaces, fell into uncovered wells or were attacked by wild animals, suggesting an absence of adult supervision. Yes, many children died of diseases not then treatable, but also from easily preventable causes.

Beginning in the early nineteenth century, parental attitudes and behavior began to shift. More affluent parents kept children at home, in school and away from work. An array of new institutions, including expanded schools, orphanages, and children's hospitals, gradually emerged to protect and enhance children's welfare. Progress was real, but slow and uneven. For example, the overwhelming majority of nineteenth-century American autobiographies report children being disciplined with a cane, paddle or leather strap (Pleck, 1987). Child abuse and neglect became criminal offenses starting only in the 1870s. Mandatory schooling did not become universal until the early twentieth century. The United States abolished child labor only in 1938.

Slowly, protecting children from harm became a public priority. Indeed, the growth of the American welfare state, from Aid to Dependent Children in the

1930s to Head Start, established in 1965, was largely driven by concern for children's well-being. This effort to ensure a 'right to childhood,' free from abuse or exploitation, reflected a growing consensus that children, by virtue of their special vulnerability, deserved public support.

Unfortunately, in recent decades, collective concern has often given way to something more inward looking. Typically, parents have responded to threats to children's well-being in one of two unhelpful ways: By overestimating the risk and focusing exclusively on safeguarding their own children, or discounting the danger, telling themselves it can't happen to their kids. These responses are especially easy when the problems seem to be disproportionately confined to poor children or those of another nation. Today, there is a tendency for many affluent parents to view their children as beings to be protected and projects to be perfected and to regard other children as potential problems to be avoided. As a result, more American moms and dads drive their kids to school, producing congestion in school zones that actually endangers children. Parents discourage their children from roaming freely outdoors, contributing to obesity and excessive time spent in front of screens. Instead of translating their fears into a communal response – for example, by increasing supervision at parks and playgrounds – parents react to their worries on an individual basis, to the detriment of all children's well-being.

A key question is whether affluent parents will respond to the challenges of inequality in childhood with pity and a shrug of the shoulders, or as a call to arms demanding concerted collective action and a deepening commitment to children's welfare, irrespective of nationality, class, ethnicity, race, and gender.

Disclosure statement

No potential conflict of interest was reported by the author.

References

Calvert, K. (1992). *Children in the house: The material culture of early childhood, 1600–1800*. Boston, MA: Northeastern University Press.

Chudacoff, H. P. (1989). *How old are you? Age consciousness in American culture*. Princeton, NJ: Princeton University Press.

Chudacoff, H. P. (2007). *Children at play: An American History*. New York, NY: NYU Press.

Cross, G. (1999). *Kids' stuff: Toys and the changing world of American childhood*. Cambridge, MA: Harvard University Press.

Davies, L. (1995). Babies co-sleeping with parents. *Midwives: Official Journal of the Royal College of Midwives, 108*, 384–386.

Furedi, F. (2001). *Paranoid parenting: Abandon your anxieties and be a good parent*. London: Allen Lane.

Golden, J., Meckel, R. A., Richard, A., & Prescott, H. M. P. (Eds.). (2004). *Children and youth in sickness and in health: A historical handbook and guide*. Westport, CT: Greenwood Press.

Gordon, L., & McLanahan, S. (1991). Single parenthood in 1900. *Journal of Family History, 16*, 97–116.

Hardyment, C. (2007). *Dream babies: Childcare advice from John Locke to Gina Ford*. London: Francis Lincoln.

Hrdy, S. B. (2009). *Mothers and others: The evolutionary origins of mutual understanding*. Cambridge, MA: Belknap Press of Harvard University Press.

Hulbert, A. (2003). *Raising America: Experts, parents and a century of advice about children*. New York, NY: Knopf.

Kline, D. T. Holding therapy. (1998, March 7). History-child-family listserv (history-child-family@mailbase.ac.uk)

Lancy, D. F. (2011, February 15). Talking trash or taking it out? *Psychology Today*. Retrieved from https://www.psychologytoday.com/blog/benign-neglect/201102/talking-trash-or-taking-it-out

LeVine, R. A., & LeVine, S. (2016). *Do parents matter? Why Japanese babies sleep soundly, Mexican siblings don't fight, and American families should just relax*. New York, NY: Public Affairs.

Maier, T. (1998). *Dr. Spock: An American life*. New York, NY: Harcourt Brace.

Mintz, S. (2004). *Huck's Raft: A History of American Childhood*. Cambridge, MA: Belknap Press of Harvard University Press.

Pleck, E. (1987). *Domestic tyranny: The making of American social policy against family violence from colonial times to the present*. New York, NY: Oxford University Press.

Rothschild, J. (2005). *The dream of the perfect child*. Bloomington, IN: Indiana University Press.

Schultz, J. A. (1995). *The knowledge of childhood in the German middle ages, 1100–1350*. Philadelphia, PA: University of Pennsylvania Press.

Stearns, P. N. (2003). *Anxious parents: A history of modern childrearing in America*. New York, NY: New York University Press.

Children and emotions history

Peter N. Stearns

ABSTRACT
This paper explores two major sets of changes in American approaches to children and emotion, around 1800 and again in the 1920s; and then examines more specific shifts in emotions such as grief, happiness and shame, exploring causation and impact. The text sketches several key historical findings about emotional standards and childhood, particularly in the USA, while indicating as well some characteristic challenges and opportunities for further work. The presentation also interweaves two other issues: the complexities around discussing changes and continuities in the actual emotions of children, and links – existing and potential – between historical and psychological work in the field.

Both emotions history and the history of childhood have gained ground impressively as research fields. They were of course linked early on, for example in the work of American colonial historians like John Demos, Michael Zuckerman and Philip Greven, and there have been important developments since (Demos, 1998, 1986, 2000; Greven, 1988; Zuckerman, 1982). At the same time, there are some obvious barriers to a full picture of emotions in the history of childhood.

The key problem involves evidence. All emotions history faces the challenge of trying to figure out what 'real' emotional experience in the past was, as opposed to recommended standards and representations. The challenge is obviously greater for children, who leave so few direct records on any subject. We know far more, as a result, about what emotional standards adults sought for children, than about children's own emotional values, much less their 'real' experience. Diary evidence; direct records of children's emotional terms – for example, introduction of the word 'sissy' in the nineteenth-century to denote unduly fearful boys; and particularly for the twentieth-century and beyond, observational studies – provide genuine entry, as the exploration of specific emotional changes will suggest. But there are undeniable gaps (Frevert, 2012; Frevert et al., 2014; Matt & Stearns, 2014).

Issues of social class also loom large. Emotions historians have had far more success, for obvious reasons, in dealing with upper- or middle-class standards than with those of other groups, though there are a few exceptions. This deserves serious attention going forward, as it overlaps with similar constraints in the history of childhood (Stearns, 2003). The subject is complicated also by geographical unevenness, with scholarship on the U.S.A and Western Europe better developed than work on other regions, despite some significant research in Chinese history (Kinney, 1995).

One other distraction slowed efforts in the emotions history of childhood, though I think the field has now recovered. The generalizations offered by Philippe Ariès helped launch serious work on the history of childhood but also drew exaggerated contrasts between traditional and modern patterns (Ariès, 1962; Pollock, 1983, 1987). This triggered a debate between historians who might claim that premodern families avoided emotional attachments between parents and children, and specialists who responded by overemphasizing continuities (Stone, 1977). More recent work has operated in between these two extremes, encouraged by parallel research in psychology – as suggested in Paul Harris' paper – that notes the importance of cultural variables in determining aspects of emotional experience.

What follows offers, first, a tentative overall sketch, highlighting two points of overall change in the emotional framework for American childhood, or at least middle-class childhood, and raising the possibility of a third. I then turn to more focused explorations of particular emotional shifts, most of which fit within the larger pattern; this approach allows richer discussions of causation and, particularly, results in terms of expectations and actual emotional experience alike, plus firmer attention to historical interactions with psychology. The emphasis is on significant changes, which is where I believe emotions historians make their greatest interdisciplinary contribution, and on cases where societal shifts combined with new cultural signals, affecting adults dealing with children and sometimes children themselves.

Subperiods in modern American emotions

The largest transformations in American emotional history are associated with developments in the later eighteenth/early nineteenth centuries. Cultural redefinitions are heavily involved. This was the point at which American advice literature began clearly to assimilate the reevaluation of children's nature initially associated with figures like John Locke and Rousseau. While evangelical Protestant groups worked to hang on to traditions, mainstream Protestantism moved away from emphasis on original sin, toward beliefs in children as lovable innocents. At least for adults, individualism gained new emphasis

(Eustace, 2008), and this could translate – at least gradually – into new socialization goals for children – reducing for example a purely customary reliance on obedience (Demos, 1998, 1986, 2000; Greven, 1988; Zuckerman, 1982).

Changes in structure paralleled the cultural shifts. Birth rates began to go down, and this at least raised important questions about adult emotional investments in children and about some aspects of children's own emotional experience. With work moving outside the home, the economic functions of families in some ways declined; and children began to turn from their traditional service as economic assets, contributing to the family economy at least in later childhood, into clear liabilities. All of this raised challenging questions about what the modern family was for. Responses included some striking new emotional expectations and demands. Families began to be imagined in more actively favorable emotional terms, and children began to pick up new emotional responsibilities as part of this adaptation. Here, clearly, is where responses to modern social and economic structures linked with the concomitant cultural redefinitions. The results would play out in emotional standards and at least some measurable aspects of experience through the nineteenth-century and beyond (Lasch, 1977; Mintz, 2009).

A second change point opened up in the early twentieth-century. To some extent, it built on the earlier trends; there was no complete redefinition. Thus emphasis on children's cheerfulness and happiness, already well established, clearly intensified. Respectable parents had long been urged not to discipline children in anger. This recommendation continued, though with some increasing assumption that parents probably already knew the basic message; but children's anger was now also considered in new ways, as childrearing manuals shifted from welcoming channeled anger as part of male socialization, to substituting the term aggression as part of a larger effort to control the emotion (Stearns, 1994).

But there were some newer signals as well. Overall, this second period sought to combine a firmer belief in childhood as emotionally privileged, with the complexity of raising children capable of succeeding in an increasingly managerial economy. The rapid decline in infant mortality virtually required new considerations of children's relationship to death and grief, and here striking changes in standards surely paralleled some very real changes in children's emotional lives. Demography – still-lower birth rates plus now the death rate shift –plus growing consumerism more broadly encouraged what Viviana Zelizer has aptly termed the advent of the 'priceless' child (1985). Other concerns arose, however, about emotions, such as jealousy, that might complicate adult behavior unless appropriate socialization was applied (Jacobson, 2005).

Adding to this mix was a new kind of popularized expertise, sharply replacing, by the 1920s, the kind of humane moralism that had predominated in advice manuals during the nineteenth-century. Advice now stemmed from psychological and medical research on children, as in the work of G. Stanley Hall. At the same time, new levels of reliance on advice givers, as childrearing literature swelled American bookstores, suggested a lack of parental confidence, or at least a sense that new standards were needed to prepared children for a more complex managerial economy. Children's emotions needed more parental attention as part of preparation for a constructive adulthood– learning how to curb aggression or jealousy for example. It was at this point, for example, that behaviorists like John Watson urged new strategies to deal with issues such as children's fear. While it would be some decades before the fabled 'helicopter parent' emerged, eager among other things to take charge of their children's emotional encounters even into high school and college, the seedbed began to be prepared earlier, through the eager acceptance of new kinds of advice. The definition of parental responsibility altered significantly (Stearns, 2003).

This suggested framework – major change in the early nineteenth-century, important adjustments and adaptation in the early twentieth – offers a suggestive hypothesis, though it invites further testing. The approach challenges older studies of childrearing advice, that moved from one short-term fashion, like behaviorism, to another, and it also disputes a purely generational approach to the characteristics of children and youth. The approach clearly reflects strong reliance on prescriptive materials – on what adults, and to some extent children themselves, were being told about appropriate and inappropriate emotions. The ensuing cases studies will help explore the extent to which change also entered emotional experience, though this further task invites additional work.

Love and grief: two initial cases of change

We know that urban, middle-class families in the USA began reducing their birth rate from the late eighteenth-century onward. The result could increase the amount of attention, including emotional attention, given to individual children, particularly by mothers. It might also increase a sense of emotional investment in the individual child. At the same time, chronologically, predominant childrearing literature began placing growing emphasis on parental, especially maternal affection. It also began to counsel systematically against using anger and fear in child discipline. It is not easy to disaggregate cultural and demographic causation (Cott, 1977; Stearns, 1994). Similar questions can of course be raised about the emotional repercussions of other settings where birth rates declined, as in Western Europe around the same time, East Asia more recently. While it is easy to describe the changes in prescriptive literature around more loving parent-child relations, assessing actual emotional results for children is more problematic. Some diary evidence, however, at least from later in the century suggests that many children did pick up on the loving maternal image, and responded in kind (Stearns & Weber, 1983). The changes involved also deserve assessment in terms of attachment theory, as explored in other essays in this volume.

Example 2 continues the demography theme, but with more directly measurable emotional results. Between 1880 and 1920, in the USA as in Western Europe, infant and child mortality began to decline dramatically. The result clearly prompted further emotional reevaluations of individual children, now almost certain to survive. And it had direct impact on grief standards, both in general and concerning children particularly. Victorian culture had paid great and in many ways sympathetic attention to grief, as part of the family emotional experience and an outgrowth of greater expectations of love. In the 1870s, grief kits were available for girls, as part of the paraphernalia associated with dolls: one could buy mourning clothes, even a casket for dolls, on grounds that girls should be sensitized to their future roles in helping to guide familial grief. By the 1920s however this equation was stood on its head. Experts and popularizers now urged that grief was far too strong an emotion for children to bear; they should be kept away from it, possibly removed from funerals altogether. New words should replace crass references to death: children might be told that a grandparent has 'passed' or was simply 'through.' And of course the actual opportunities for grief did decline, as fewer and fewer children experienced loss of sibling. Grief became a more remote emotion, all the more in that parents often went to great extremes to protect children from the encounter – sometimes even in dealing with the deaths of household pets (Stearns, 2007). Declining exposure to death and grief formed a measurable change in children's actual emotional experience, though this could also lead to confusion when death did intrude.

Jealousy: a more challenging case

The demographic transition and the rise of schooling raises at least one question for the emotional experience of childhood, given the decline in the number of siblings and partial substitution of age-based friendships (Rosenzweig, 1999; Rotundo, 1993). Within this framework, jealousy was urgently reevaluated.

The 1920s featured unprecedented concerns about problems of sibling rivalry – an issue virtually undiscussed for the nineteenth-century. Childrearing manuals devoted large sections to sibling rivalry, and the same was true for the new journal *Parents' Magazine*. The challenge was presented in crisis terms: the arrival of a new baby could trigger emotions in the toddler sibling that demanded the most urgent attention. There was direct danger to the new baby itself: sibling rivalry could lead to direct physical violence or at least persistent conflict. There was danger as well in the larger emotional trajectory of attention should be paid to potential provocations. Grandparents, for example, must be urged to bring gifts for the affected child. Untreated jealousy would 'fester,' leading to adults that were incapable of successful family relationships and, sometimes, unable to work to their potential as well. Happily, there were remedies available. Parental watchfulness was crucial. Toddlers should be urged to talk out their jealous responses, defusing the emotion amid parental understanding. Careful gifts for the toddler as well as for the baby might allow consumer delight to overcome jealousy. The message, finally, hit home: by the 1930s parents were reporting that their own concerns about sibling rivalry constituted one of the top two problems confronted (Stearns, 1989).

What was going on here, with an emotional issue that, while surely not entirely new, had rarely assumed these proportions? The obvious component was new expertise. The 1920s saw the rise of social workers and psychologists eager to apply new expert research to issues of childhood, emotions included. From expertise to popularization, particularly the kind of popularization that could claim to be addressing vital problems that traditional parenting had ignored, was a fairly easy step. But why were parents open to this kind of expertise? Two related possibilities can be suggested, though not definitively tested. First, in an atmosphere of increasing socialization between men and women (at coeducational schools, in adult partying) control of jealousy (particularly for men) assumed new importance. Transferring this need to childhood, even if not entirely consciously, may have been an easy step: children did indeed require jealousy training different from that their parents had received. The second possibility takes us back to sibling issue. With lower birth rates, with increasingly nuclear families as both grandparents and live-in servants departed (crucial changes from the 1920s onward), battles for parental and particularly maternal affection may well have taken on new dimensions in fact, and not just in researcher fancy. Parents faced, in this regard, emotional issues their own parents had not faced, and this opened them to the new advice.

How much was children's actual emotional experience affected by all this? Surely emotional relations among siblings were influenced by new adult interventions and concerns. By the 1930s it was revealing that American adolescents were in the main eager to claim that they did not experience jealousy, that this was a childish emotion that should be firmly under control with greater maturity. While the frenzy over sibling rivalry ultimately subsided, the historical precedent helps explain findings by scholars like Peter Salovey, concerning Americans' distinctive inclination to conceal jealousy even more recently (Salovey, 1991).

The cheerful child

Another shift in the emotional expectations surrounding childhood combines demographic change – the falling birth rate – with other changes in the structures surrounding childhood but also with another set of broader cultural shifts.

The focus is once again on the first two thirds of the nineteenth-century, when what Steven Mintz has called the 'middle-class child' was being constructed (Mintz, 2009). From the early 1800s onward, beginning from very low levels, references to 'cheerful obedience' rose quite steadily in American usage, as charted by Google books. The combination had been virtually unknown in the eighteenth century, when obedience alone sufficed. Now, however, parents were encouraged to want children not only to do as they were told, but to seem happy about it – intensifying emotional demands on children themselves. Revealingly, growing use of an essentially new word (sulky, which entered the language only in the eighteenth-century) charted some aspects of resultant response. Children who complied with adult instructions but failed to show the desired smiles needed a new term, and its use grew steadily for several decades (Stearns, 2014).

Why cheerful obedience? First, obedience was a hallowed quality expected of children, so its use long persisted; only in the final decades of the nineteenth-century did obedience of any sort command less attention. But now that middle-class children were no longer expected to work, at least until adolescence, obedience in the home may have mattered less than it once did (school settings were another matter). By the same token, however, as children moved from being economic assets to clear liabilities, families at least implicitly confronted the dilemma of what children were for. Contribution to a positive vision of the family was arguably the answer; and this is where cheerfulness could seem increasingly important. Emphasis on cheer and happiness was rising in Western and particularly American culture generally, so a translation into the family setting was not surprising. The link to obedience constituted a first cut at defining the new expectations for children. Again, functional changes and cultural signals combined (Stearns, 2014).

And the emphasis continued. Childrearing literature in the interwar decades was filled with titles or chapter headings reflecting the imperative of good cheer (now separated from obedience). Birthday celebrations, gaining ground steadily as emotional events in childhood, focused strongly on the happiness theme. The song, Happy Birthday, was introduced in fact in 1926, and by the following decade had become a cultural staple. The push toward happiness, and consumerist versions thereof, also led by mid-century to a measurable increase in children's capacity to recognize, and complain about, boredom, another important twentieth-century change (Kotchemidova, 2005).

Here then is a case of significant emotional change, measurable to a point, and if anything overdetermined by the factors, both structural and cultural, that contributed. Assessment, however, is another matter: what was the actual result in terms of children's emotions? Connections with consumerism, both adult provision and children's own expectations, are virtually certain. It is easy enough to find direct twentieth-century evidence of children's open happiness in the presence of consumer goods, as in the high valuation of birthdays with their abundance of 'cards and gifts' (Alexander, 2012, p. 139). By the later nineteenth-century, children were also being urged to smile more, an impulse that has clearly persisted. Difficulties with sadness in childhood – for children themselves and for adults involved – deserve more exploration. Comparative issues are also inviting: to what extent did American example, or parallel causation, affect childhood emotion in other contemporary societies?

Envy: a more focused case

If the link between children's happiness and rising American consumerism is diffuse, though probable, examination of envy makes the connection quite clear. Again structural shifts – the obvious growth of a consumer economy in the later nineteenth century, complete with new practices such as allowances for children – and cultural changes – in this instance, religious adjustments – combine. But in this instance, changes in economic context preceded the adaptation of recommended emotional standards.

Adult consumerism gained ground rapidly in the USA by the end of the nineteenth century. Children had abundant evidence around them of the emotional satisfactions their parents and adult neighbors seemed to gain from acquiring new objects, and they often had parents who found it increasingly logical to express their love by buying toys and other gifts. And they had peers who were eager to show off their own acquisitions. Stanley Hall reported in 1903 on children's eagerness to use material objects as a source of boasting: 'My sled is better than yours. Yours was made. Mine was bought' (1911).

In this situation consumer envy undoubtedly gained ground as part of children's emotional experience. Various observers reported on a growing tendency for children to lie about their possessions. Pressures on parents to help the child keep up with school fashion or other targets mounted steadily. Ultimately these developments overwhelmed more traditional advice to children to keep greed in check. After 1915 a new generation of child-rearing experts shifted gears, and not only accepted envy but even encouraged it as a spur to adjustments to the modern world. Intelligent and discriminating consumerism was now a valid goal, and appropriate doses of envy – including aspirations for higher-quality goods – could play a constructive role here. The good parent would not waste time discouraging envy, but would keep it in bounds by satisfying some of the child's consumer goals (Cross, 2004; Hall & Smith, 1903; Matt, 2002).

Shame: a final case

Shame, a more complex and diffuse emotion than envy, provides one final case study where significant change can be explored, but in this instance also in a broader and more comparative geographical context.

Agricultural societies seem uniformly to have depended heavily on shame, though available evidence varies by region. For children, shame helped confirm the emphasis on obedience; it also, at least in principle, aligned children with community standards. Shame had the merit as well of reducing reliance on physical punishments – in policing generally, and in childrearing specifically.

Socialization for shame began early. We have particularly good evidence, in the Agricultural Age, from China from the Han dynasty onward, and for colonial North America. In both cases many parents responded to childish bad behavior by denying access and affection for a period of time, turning away from the child's laments. The goal was to associate misbehavior with withdrawal of love and of community, so that the child would learn to avoid this deprivation in future and in later life. Shame, in other words, was designed to punish, but also to serve as ongoing deterrent. Contemporary psychologists like June Tangney and Michael Lewis warn of shame's toxicity, its capacity to destroy self-worth and produce not remediation, but either despair or defiance (Lewis, 1992; Tangney, Stuewig, & Mashek, 2007). Without disputing these results for the contemporary West, it is possible to suggest that the kind of shaming current in more traditional societies was not so uniformly devastating, Properly socialized, children could learn to avoid it or, if affected, realize that the situation could be repaired.

In the U.S.A, and in Western Europe though possibly with some lag, shame was decisively revisited in the late 18th and early 19th centuries. The change was most obvious in penology: classic shaming devices, like the public stocks, were debated and abolished – in Massachusetts, as early as 1804. The reasons? Public shaming was incompatible with individual dignity – it was, in the terms of the new American constitution, a cruel and unusual punishment (Stearns, in press).

Tracing the attacks on shame in childrearing are slightly more difficult – there was no symbol to compare with the stocks. But the shift did occur. By the 1830s and 1840s mainstream childrearing advice insisted that children be disciplined carefully, with as much emphasis on positive motivation as possible. They should not be encouraged to think of themselves as bad individuals. Many manuals advised against shaming directly, because of the harm it did to a child's mental state. By the 1870s, manuals went on to identify the importance of self-esteem – the term was used directly – in opposition to shaming. A new framework was being set that would in many ways simply expand over ensuing decades (Child, 1831).

The turn against shame in childrearing obviously raises several analytical issues. Causation is one. Why would childrearing advisors turn against a disciplinary emotion that had so long served as a staple? American society was beginning to urbanize at this point, and some analysts have argued that the decline of cohesive village communities would inevitably doom a reliance on shame. This argument, however, does not work: for East Asian societies, as they urbanized, would continue to rely on high levels of shame, simply turning the emotion more fully toward motivating academic achievement in children. The American answer must rest more on cultural shifts. With beliefs in original sin increasingly abandoned, with individualism and individual dignity increasingly emphasized, with new expectations of children in the family and in society more generally, heavy reliance on shaming simply no longer made sense. A new type of child was being sought, and emotional guidelines had to be reconsidered in the process.

Of course shame was not fully excised. Quite apart from the challenge of figuring out actual parental responses to the new standards, shame continued to operate in the schools. The famous dunce cap – first explicitly mentioned in Britain in 1840 – continued to be used to shame poor-performing students in front of their classmates well into the nineteenth-century. Shame seemed essential to teachers particularly as reliance on corporal punishment was restricted; and many female teachers, worried about their inability physically to intimidate older boys, also mentioned their reliance on shame. For many children, implicitly shielded from much shame in early childhood but then exposed to schooling, the emotional results may have been somewhat confusing (Kaestle, 1978).

The campaign against shaming in childhood continued, however, into the later nineteenth-century. Not only were parents still warned; classic shaming devices in the schools were phased out, and instances in which teachers too blatantly shame a child now brought fierce parental and community response. Shame was not eliminated, but it was more consistently downplayed for children. At the same time, from the 1960s onward, massive programs to boost children's self-esteem provided an alternative focus, that would indeed work to increase resentment against any shaming efforts that did occur (Stout, 2000).

The result raises several final issues, where history joins with other types of emotional analysis, including of course psychology. Were certain children, and groups of children, still shamed in schools, if somewhat more subtly – and with what effects? Did other types of motivation work as well as shame? Comparisons with East Asian societies, where children learn to identify shame at an earlier age than in the USA and are still exposed to shame in home and school alike, are particularly revealing.

And one unexpected twist, to add to this kind of interdisciplinary analysis: shaming began to increase again in American society after the 1960s. At the very least, different groups of Americans began to differ strongly about the validity of shaming (particularly of course when the issue was shaming other people). And some American parents began, after 2000, to introduce new methods of shaming misbehaving children: requiring them to wear demeaning signs in public, cutting their hair, and even putting shaming messages about them on social media. This aspect of children's emotional history continues to evolve. And historians can join with other disciplines in assessing the new complexity.

Conclusion

Traced across two periods of major changes – the early nineteenth-century and the mid-20th, several highly probable shifts in children's emotional experience emerge – despite the lack of systematic direct evidence. Increases in opportunities for open envy, reductions in the experience of grief or shame, heighted expectations of happiness and resultant resentment of boredom, and new tensions around jealousy are supported by considerable clusters of data.

Increased parental efforts to intermediate for children around certain emotional issues can also be traced.

The results also feed a robust relationship between emotions history and psychology, in several ways. The historical data strongly emphasize the importance of cultural factors, and cultural change, as against an over-rigid evolutionary approach, meshing with Paul Harris' overall argument. Further, historical assessments interact with key findings in psychology, as in Salovey's comparative work on jealousy or the now-dominant concerns about the results of shame, presenting opportunities for further interdisciplinary work in exploring resulting complexities and in dealing as well with issues such as social class or comparative patterns.

One final challenge emerges as well, where historical analysis might readily combine with psychological data and insight: when, and on what basis, will a new period emerge, adjusting prior patterns inherited form the transition of the twentieth-century? Links with the past abound, as in the emotionally anxious helicopter parent. But do the increases in childhood anxiety and depression, recorded in more recent decades, suggest a new set of factors as well? Is there a set of cultural and structural shifts that can be compared to the change elements that emerged around 1800, and again in the 1920s? The question is classically historical, but the contemporaneity, and the importance, of the issues invite interdisciplinary collaboration as well.

Disclosure statement

No potential conflict of interest was reported by the author.

References

Alexander, K. (2012, Summer). Can the girl guide speak? The perils and pleasures of looking for children's voices in archival research. *Jeunesse Young People, Texts, Cultures, 4*, 132–145.

Ariès, P. (1962). *Centuries of childhood: A social history of family life*. New York, NY: Vintage Books.

Child, L. (1831). *The mother's book*. Boston, MA: Carter, Hendee and Babcock. Accessed from HathiTrust.

Cott, N. F. (1977). *The bonds of womanhood: 'Woman's sphere' in New England, 1780–1835*. New Haven, CT: Yale University Press.

Cross, G. (2004). *The cute and the cool wondrous innocence and modern American children's culture*. New York, NY: Oxford University Press.

Demos, J. (1986). *Past present and personal: The family and the life course in American history*. New York, NY: Oxford University Press.

Demos, J. (1988). Shame and guilt in early New England. In C. Z. Stearns & P. N. Stearns (Eds.), *Emotion and social change: Toward a new psychohistory*. New York, NY: Holmes and Meier.

Demos, J. (2000). *A little commonwealth: Family life in Plymouth colony*. New York, NY: Oxford University Press.

Eustace, N. (2008). *Passion is the gale: Emotion, power, and the coming of the American revolution*. Chapel Hill: University of North Carolina Press.

Frevert, U. (2012, Summer). Can the girl guide speak? The perils and pleasures of looking for children's voices in archival research. *Jeunesse: Young People, Texts, Cultures, 4*, 132–145.

Frevert, U., Eitler, P., Olsen, S., Jensen, U., Pernau, M., Bruckenhaus, D., ... Haberlen, J. C. (Eds.). (2014). *Learning how to feel: Children's literature and emotional socialization*. Oxford: Oxford University Press.

Greven, P. J. (1988). *The protestant temperament: Patterns of child-rearing, religious experience, and the self in early America*. Chicago, IL: University of Chicago Press.

Hall, S. G. (1911). *Adolescence*, Vol. 2. New York, NY: D. Appleton.

Hall, S. G., & Smith, T. (1903). Showing off and bashfulness as phases of self-consciousness. *Pedagogical Seminary, 1–0*, 172–173.

Jacobson, L. (2005). *Raising consumers: Children and the American mass market in the early twentieth century*. New York, NY: Columbia University Press.

Kaestle, C. F. (1978, SUmmer). Social change, discipline, and the common school in early nineteenth-century America'. *The Journal of Interdisciplinary History, 9*, 1–17.

Kinney, A. B. (1995). *Chinese views of childhood*. Honolulu: University of Hawaii Press.

Kinney, A. B. (2004). *Representations of childhood and youth in early China*. Stanford, CA: Stanford University Press.

Kotchemidova, C. (2005). From good cheer to 'drive-by smiling': A social history of cheerfulness. *Journal of Social History, 39*, 5–37.

Lasch, C. (1977). *Haven in a heartless word: The family besieged*. New York, NY: Basic Books.

Lewis, M. (1992). *Shame: The exposed self*. New York, NY: Free Press.

Matt, S. (2002). *Keeping up with the Joneses: Envy in American Consumer Society, 1890–1930*. Philadelphia, PA: University of Pennsylvania Press.

Matt, S. J., & Stearns, P. N. (Eds.). (2014). *Doing emotions history*. Urbana: University of Illinois Press.

Mintz, S. (2009). *Huck's raft: A history of American childhood*. Ann Arbor: University of Michigan.

Pollock, L. A. (1983). *Forgotten children: Parent–child relations from 1500 to 1900*. New York, NY: Cambridge University Press.

Pollock, L. A. (1987). *A lasting relationship: Parents and children over three centuries*. Hanover: University Press of New England.

Rosenzweig, L. W. (1999). *Another self: Middle-class American women and their friends in the twentieth century*. New York, NY: New York University Press.

Rotundo, A. (1993). *American manhood: Transformations in masculinity from the revolution to the modern era*. New York, NY: Basic Books.

Salovey, P. (1991). *The psychology of jealousy and envy*. New York, NY: The Guilford Press.

Stearns, P. N. (1989). *Jealousy: The evolution of an emotion in American history*. New York: New York University Press.

Stearns, P. N. (1994). *American cool: Constructing a twentieth-century emotional style*. New York: New York University Press.

Stearns, P. N. (2003). *Anxious parents: A history of modern childrearing in America*. New York: New York University Press.

Stearns, P. N. (2007). *Revolutions in sorrow: The American experience of death in global perspective*. Boulder, CO: Paradigm.

Stearns, P. N. (2014). Obedience and emotion: A challenge in the emotional history of childhood. *Journal of Social History, 47*, 593–611.

Stearns, P. N. (2016). *A history of shame*. Champaign, IL: University of Illinois Press.

Stearns, P. N., & Weber, M. P. (Eds.). (1983). *The spencers of amberson avenue: A turn-of-the-century memoir*. Pittsburgh, PA: University of Pittsburgh Press.

Stone, L. (1977). *The family, sex and marriage in England, 1500–1800*. New York, NY: Harper and Row. ACLS Humanities E-Book.

Stout, M. (2000). *The feel-good curriculum: The dumbing-down of America's kids in the name of self-esteem*. Cambridge, MA: Perseus Books.

Tangney, J. P., Stuewig, J., & Mashek, D. J. (2007). Moral emotions and moral behavior. *Annual Review of Psychology*, 58, 345–372. http://www.ncbi,nlm.nih.gov/pmc/articles/PMC3083636/

Zelizer, V. (1985). *Pricing the priceless child: The changing social value of children*. New York, NY: Basic Books.

Zuckerman, M. (1982). *Friends and neighbors: Group life in America's first plural society*. Philadelphia, PA: Temple University Press.

Emotion, imagination and the world's furniture

Paul L. Harris

ABSTRACT
I scrutinize a view of emotion that was established in the late nineteenth century and bequeathed to subsequent generations of psychological researchers. That view has strong evolutionary undertones so that continuities between humans and other animals have guided psychological research on emotion – both with children and with adults. At the center of this biological view is the idea that an emotion is a set or facial and bodily reactions triggered by a first-hand encounter with a situation of some biological significance – a potential danger, a separation from a caregiver, a sudden noise, or a snake. I argue that such a view obscures two species-specific features of human emotion: (i) the extent to which the emotional valence of a given encounter is signaled by the culture rather than by any intrinsic features; (ii) the ways in which emotion is driven not by first-hand encounters with the world's furniture but by mental encounters that depend on the human imagination. These two features offer a helpful framework for thinking about the history of emotions as well as their development in childhood.

In his autobiography, the English developmental psychologist, James Sully recalls a memorable encounter one wet Sunday afternoon in 1876 (Sully, 1918). He had gone to have tea at the Priory, London home of the polymath G. H. Lewes and his partner, Marian Evans – better known as George Eliot. Finding himself the sole remaining guest, Sully was about to leave when the maid entered and announced the arrival of two distinguished visitors: 'Mr. and Mrs. Darwin.' Lewes encouraged Sully not to leave and the conversation turned to the recently published first issue of a new journal – *Mind*. Darwin spoke in praise of the journal and, not fully realizing whom he was addressing, added that he had particularly enjoyed an article on 'Physiological Psychology in Germany.' Lewes smilingly explained to Darwin that he was conversing with the author of that very article – James Sully.

We do not know if the ensuing conversation touched on developmental psychology or the question of whether the new journal might be used as a vehicle to promote that nascent discipline; but soon after this encounter, Darwin submitted a paper to *Mind*. Under the title 'Biographical sketch of an infant', he gathered together a variety of notes and observations that he had made some 37 years earlier on the early development of his son, Charles, known in the family as Doddy. The article was published a few months later in the July issue of *Mind* in 1877. It stands as a pioneering attempt to analyze early psychological development and in subsequent issues of *Mind* several other reports of infant psychology were published (Shuttleworth, 2013).

Some of the material in Darwin's article echoed themes that he had examined a few years earlier in *The Expression of the Emotions in Man and Animals* (Darwin, 1872). That book, with its emphasis on continuities between human beings and other animals and its focus on the facial expression of emotion – in infants as well as adults – has had a major impact on the psychological study of emotion. In the twentieth century, the work of Paul Ekman, did a great deal to sustain and promote interest in the facial expression of emotion and Ekman himself paid tribute to Darwin's contribution by editing a new edition of Darwin's book, with an introduction and various annotations (Ekman & Darwin, 2009). Today, we continue to see fierce debate about the universality of facial expressions of emotion – and more generally about the existence of so-called basic emotions (Barrett, 2011; Russell, 1994).

Not long after Darwin's article, in 1884, *Mind* published another landmark contribution to the psychology of emotion, this time from across the Atlantic. William James asked: 'What is an emotion?' In a well-known passage, he invited readers to consider various emotionally charged situations from a common sense standpoint: 'Common sense says, we lose our fortune, are sorry and weep; we meet a bear, are frightened and run; we are insulted by a rival, are angry and strike.' He went on to insist, however, that common sense misinterprets the actual sequence of events – the more rational claim is that 'we feel sorry because we cry, angry because we strike, afraid because we tremble.' On this view, our experience of emotion is constituted by our registration of the various bodily changes that are triggered when we encounter an emotionally charged situation. Indeed, if those bodily changes did not occur, we would experience, at most, a colorless, cognitive state stripped of genuine emotion.

These several early contributions to the psychology of emotion eventually led to a successful, albeit contentious, research program with three notable features. First, in line with Darwin's continuity thesis, parallels between human beings and other animals were emphasized rather than major discontinuities. Second, the reflections of Darwin and James led to an emphasis on the various rapid changes, whether in the face or the body, that are associated with an emotion. Indeed, those reflections set the stage for tracking down the distinctive and potentially universal facial or bodily signature thought to be linked to each supposedly basic emotion – such as fear, anger, joy, disgust and so forth. Third, almost as a matter of course, some of the guiding assumptions laid out by James with respect to the elicitation of emotion have endured unchallenged. This latter point warrants more detailed analysis for it will be central to my own emphasis on the distinctive nature of human emotion.

The world's furniture

James invites his readers to remember that: 'The nervous system of every living thing is but a bundle of predispositions to react in particular ways upon contact of particular features of the environment.' Citing the examples of a hound tracking a fox, or a hen brooding on an egg, he moves on to instances of emotional reactions:

> The love of a man for woman, or of the human for her babe, our wrath at snakes, and our fear of precipices may all be described similarly, as instances of the way in which peculiarly conformed pieces of the world's furniture will fatally call forth most particular mental and bodily reactions, in advance of, and often in direct opposition to, the verdict of our deliberate reason upon them.

Doffing his intellectual hat to the relevance of evolutionary thinking, James goes on to claim that Darwin and his successors are 'only just beginning to reveal the 'universal parasitism' of these emotional reactions.

Many subsequent studies of emotion, including studies of emotional development in childhood, subscribe to this view, with its implication that human beings everywhere and at all times are ineluctably disposed to respond with particular emotions – love, anger, fear – to selected pieces of the world's furniture. For example, Ekman deployed this same notion in his cross-cultural studies of emotion. His research program is generally regarded as focusing on the facial expression of emotion and that is certainly correct. At the same time, in order to test participants' perception of emotion in other cultures, he selected a particular situation – for example, the arrival of friends or an encounter with something that smells bad – and asked participants to indicate – from among a set of facial expressions – which of them would ordinarily be elicited by such a situation (Ekman & Friesen, 1971). Similarly, when asking participants to deliberately simulate the facial expression of a given emotion, Ekman asked them to show how they would look if they encountered a variety of emotionally charged situations (Ekman, 1973). In short, Ekman's work, like that of James and Darwin, assumes the existence not just of universal facial expressions but of universal elicitors of those expressions – pieces of the world's furniture that have the same emotional impact in all cultures and at all times. Similar remarks can be made about classic studies of emotional development. For example, in his grand survey of fear reactions in young children, Bowlby cites a variety of biologically prepared elicitors, including sudden loud noises, darkness, snakes, heights, strangers and so forth (Bowlby, 1973). Indeed, several sustained research programs in developmental psychology have been devoted to analyzing the time-course of early emerging fears, such as fear of heights (Gibson & Walk, 1960) or fear of strangers (Lewis, 2014).

Humanist that he was, James recognizes, and spends some time working through, a potent objection to this biological, and ultimately a-cultural and a-historical, approach to human emotion. He writes: 'most of the objects of civilized man's emotions are things to which it would be preposterous to suppose their nervous systems connately adapted. Most occasions of shame and many insults are purely conventional, and vary with the social environment.' He goes on to acknowledge that in cases such as these, 'it would seem that the ideas of shame, desire, regret, etc. must first have been attached by education and association to these conventional objects...' However, sticking to his evolutionary stance, James proceeds to argue that the existence of such conventional objects does not involve any fundamental change in the nature of emotion itself. Rather, the same innate patterns of reaction are elicited but now by virtue of an encounter with 'conventional objects' rather than the 'world's furniture'. After all, he writes: 'a nervous tendency to discharge being once there, all sorts of unforeseen things may pull the trigger and let loose the effects.'

If we fully accept this doctrine, it offers somewhat disconcerting relief to scholars who might want to study the history of the emotions. It implies that, strictly speaking, there is no history to study. Admittedly, the conventional objects of our emotions – the particular social encounters that elicit shame or pride or anger – may change over time but the emotions themselves remain fixed by our biological heritage. On this view, our emotional lives in the twenty-first century are fundamentally similar to those of all our most distant human forebears even if we differ in what irks, inspires, or consoles us. Indeed, to the extent that education serves only to bring about changes in the types of conventional objects that adults – as compared to young children – recognize and respond to, then developmental psychologists of emotion can also take an indefinite vacation. If James is right the core emotional reactions of an adult are not so very different from those of a child. Again, all that changes are the objects that elicit those reactions but not the emotional reactions themselves.

My naive intuition is that, in the study of emotion, such a scholarly abandonment of history and of development is not about to happen. But are there also good intellectual reasons that it should not. What exactly is wrong with James's argument? In the end, I think his focus on the internal aspects of emotions, especially our awareness of bodily reactions, leads him to truncate the huge gap between man and animals, and between infant and adult, notably with respect to what counts as an emotionally charged encounter in the first place.

Distinctive features of human emotions

There are several intertwined features of human emotion that undermine the continuity thesis on which the account of emotion proposed by James, and ultimately by Darwin, is constructed. First, in recent decades, the standard opposition between biological and cultural approaches to human psychology has given way to a more thoughtful consideration of the ways in which human evolution did not come to end once human culture began to grow in complexity and flexibility. Instead, there was likely to have been continuing biological selection even within the adaptive terms imposed by the growth of human culture (Henrich, 2015; Richerson & Boyd, 2005). For example, in the case of tool use, there was likely to have been a shingling of cultural and biological change, notably evolutionary selection for culturally savvy individuals – those with the ability to faithfully imitate and model effective tool use. Indeed, a plethora of recent evidence shows that young children are remarkably faithful in the way that they copy demonstrations of a novel tool or strategy (Harris, 2012a). Non-human primates, by comparison, are likely to simplify the demonstration that they have observed rather than to faithfully reproduce it. Indeed, when faced with an impasse in trying to solve a practical problem, human children are much more disposed to attend to and seek guidance from a model's demonstration than are non-human primates (Herrmann, Call, Hernandez-Lloreda, Hare, & Tomasello, 2007). These tendencies imply that Mother Nature has prepared young children to enter, and become a skilled member of, a given culture with its own specific practices. To put it succinctly, human children are biologically prepared for a world that includes not just natural kinds – the world's furniture as James puts it – but also culturally specific artifacts, such as tools, procedures and rituals. Much the same can be said, of course, with respect to language. Human children are biologically prepared to enter a world that includes culturally specific modes of communication, notably the particular language – or languages – of their immediate caregivers.

What are the implications of these remarks for human emotion? First, they suggest that, even if children are born with a repertoire of relatively fixed emotional reactions, each triggered by a set of naturally occurring phenomena, they are also readily disposed to look to members of their group for guidance with respect to the emotional valence of a long list of cultural phenomena, notably the particular Gods, artifacts, and rituals that are found in the surrounding culture. Indeed, the evidence suggests that this social attentiveness is displayed not only with respect to cultural phenomena that carry no inherent emotional valence for the child, it is also displayed when children appraise the world's furniture, to borrow James's phrase once more. I offer one worked example, of the way that social learning penetrates the child's prepared emotional reactions.

The observations of Gibson and Walk (1960) showed that after a certain age, toddlers are wary of heights. Placed close to an apparent cliff, they will not venture toward it or over it, even if their mother is visible, standing beyond the cliff. Subsequent work by Campos and his colleagues showed that such behavioral wariness operates in close conjunction with a pattern of physiological reactivity. If infants are lifted and placed over a cliff, their heart rate accelerates, even if they are actually supported by a solid surface made of glass (Schwartz, Campos, & Baisel, 1973). These data fit in with the Jamesian conception of biologically prepared patterns of reaction to particular features of the environment.

However, more recent research has uncovered a role for socially guided moderation of children's reactions to heights. In an influential study, Sorce, Emde, Campos, and Klinnert (1985) asked mothers to provide guidance to their infants. As infants approached the cliff, mothers expressed either joyful encouragement or fearful discouragement via their facial and vocal expressions. The impact on infants was considerable. Those who received encouragement were very likely to advance toward their mothers whereas those who received discouragement stayed put. This phenomenon of social referencing, as it came to be known, has been well studied. We know that infants remember such guiding signals, and behave in accordance with them, even when the person who provided them is no longer present (Hornik, Risenhoover, & Gunnar, 1987). Moreover, infants are receptive to signals provided by an unfamiliar adult – and not just a familiar caregiver – at least when the unfamiliar adult appears to be the local, go-to, person for unfamiliar objects within her environs (Stenberg, 2013). Finally, toddlers' receptivity to adult guidance is especially evident when they are uncertain. For example, if they face a downward slope of intermediate steepness, they are readily receptive to the emotional signals of an adult. However, if they face a slope that is evidently too steep to negotiate or too shallow to present any difficulties, adult signals have little impact on whether they tackle the slope or not (Tamis-LeMonda et al., 2008).

As a further concrete example, consider the practice of eating food X vs. Y. Despite infants' positive as well as aversive reactions to certain tastes, what human beings are prepared to eat varies dramatically across the globe. Depending on the culture in which they are growing up, children may come to think of eating food X as disgusting and eating food Y as a source of pleasure – or the reverse. Not surprisingly, the primary way that such emotional reactions are learned is via observation. Children look to other members of their culture for guidance in what foods should be eaten and what should be avoided (Shutts, Kinzler, & DeJesus, 2013). Indeed, such culturally-guided learning has its foundations in early social experience. Monolingual (but not bilingual) 1-year-olds expect people who speak the same language to prefer the same foods (Liberman, Woodward, Sullivan, & Kinzler, 2016).

Summing up, the implication of these findings is that young children do display the kind of biologically prepared reactions that James describes but from an early age they also look to others for guidance. They are especially prone to accept that guidance when they experience uncertainty. Indeed, such guidance can, within limits, influence their reactions toward features of the world that signal danger or seem aversive. The particular emotion that they express towards a given piece of the world's furniture is critically dependent on their receptivity to guidance from others, especially those who are members of their own culture

Missing persons

As noted earlier, a great deal of research on emotion has focused on direct encounters with an emotionally-charged situation – the imminent danger of an advancing bear, the putrid smell of a rotting carcass, the unexpected return of a friend. Developmental research with young infants has taken a similar tack. Consider the widely used Strange Situation that is used to probe young children's attachment to a caregiver. At selected points in that procedure, the infant is faced with various emotionally charged situations – the approach of a stranger, the departure of the caregiver, and the eventual reunion with that same caregiver. Diagnoses of an infant's attachment are largely based on his or her emotional reactions – of wariness, distress, or joy – to these successive episodes. In that respect, the study of attachment fits in well with the evolutionary stance adopted by James and indeed by Bowlby, the leading architect of attachment theory.

However, it is important to also recognize ways in which the study of attachment has revealed how emotional development cannot be fully described in terms of the prepared and relatively fixed reactions that James emphasizes. First, and most obviously, we know that there are relatively marked and stable differences among infants in the way that they respond to the various episodes of the Strange Situation. It is not the case that all infants are wary of the approaching stranger; it is not the case that all infants express distress when their caregiver leaves; and it is not the case that all infants express joy when they are reunited with their caregiver. To the best of our knowledge, the variability in infants' reactions is at least, in part, a reflection of the expectations they have built up about their caregiver's sensitivity and availability (De Wolff & van IJzendoorn, 1997).

Further evidence for the powerful impact of such social learning has emerged from recent studies of children who have remained, for varying lengths of time, in orphanages providing minimal personalized care. Such children display long-term disturbances in their emotional appraisal and patterns of approach to unfamiliar individuals (Nelson, Fox, & Zeanah, 2014; Rutter et al., 2007). They are prone to display a pattern of indiscriminate friendliness even to people they have just met. By implication, early patterns of socialization can have marked effects on the emotional repertoire of infants, older children and adolescents. Such effects have long been studied and noted in other primates, and so in this regard, what we see in children is not confined to the emotional development of the human species.

However, another feature of attachment theory that is less obvious and indeed under-studied, points to a uniquely human disposition. As children get older, they are increasingly able to cope with short-term separations from a primary caregiver. The adjustment to day-care and preschool that is shown by the average 3- or 4-year-old attests to such flexibility. Indeed, there is evidence that 1- and 2-year-olds can cope with several days or weeks of separation from a primary caregiver, provided they have another familiar attachment figure to comfort and support them (Robertson & Robertson, 1971). A speculative but plausible interpretation of these findings, consistent with the fact that the caregiving of young infants is often distributed across multiple individuals in the human species rather than restricted to a single attachment figure (Hrdy, 2009), is that from a relatively early age, children have the cognitive resources to 'keep in mind' their connections to a variety of significant others – despite their absence (Harris, 2016). Symbolic reminders of those absent others, in the form of photographs, can provide emotional reassurance, even to toddlers and young children (Passman & Longeway, 1982). By implication, the emotional state of the young child is not regulated exclusively by encounters in the here and now – as implied by the situational elicitors that Darwin, James, and Ekman concentrate on. In the child's mind, there exists a representation of various attachment figures, and those representations can be activated, especially in the context of symbolic reminders. Indeed, young children can invoke and interact with figures that they have invented – imaginary companions who provide companionship and excitement (Taylor, 1998).

Communication and emotion

The communication of emotion in non-human primates species is typically tied to emotionally charged events in the here and now. The alarm calls of vervet monkeys, for example, allow conspecifics to anticipate specific imminent threats – such as leopards, eagles, or pythons – and to respond appropriately to such threats (Cheney & Seyfarth, 1992). In human development, the communication of emotion is qualitatively different in several important ways. First, from an early age, children do not simply emit expressive signals, be they facial expressions, or vocalizations. They build up a vocabulary of emotion terms and even 2- and 3-year-olds use those terms appropriately to report on their own emotions and those of other people. Moreover, those reports, even when they concern the self, are not always tied to current emotional reactions. Young children also talk about emotions that were felt earlier or might be felt in the future (Wellman, Harris, Banerjee, & Sinclair, 1995). Finally, and especially important, children's emotional states are increasingly driven, not by a first-hand encounter with an event – such as a loss or threat – but by their ability to mentally represent such events in their imagination. This last point is especially important for understanding the distinctive feature of human emotion.

First, in the context of pretend play, children imagine and respond to emotionally charged situations. They invent imaginary threats, losses, and victories and they react with the appropriate emotions – anxiety, distress, or pride – to those situations. This is not likely to be due to any confusion between the imaginary and the real because even 3- and 4-year-olds are quite lucid about the difference between what they have imagined and what is real (Harris, 2000).

Similarly, in listening to stories, children become sufficiently absorbed in the fictional world that the situations that the protagonist encounters elicit emotions in them. They share in the distress, anger or joy of the protagonist (Alexander, Miller, & Hengst, 2001).

Second, in the context of everyday communication, children can learn, via the testimony of other people, about situations that are directly relevant to their own well-being or to the well-being of those that are dear to them – the unexpected death of a pet, the current illness of a grandparent, or a forthcoming visit to see cousins (Harris, 2012a). Thanks to their ability to mentally represent those situations, they are likely to react with emotion – to feel sad, worried, or excited by what they have been told. Note that in such cases, children need have no direct, first-hand evidence of the situation being reported. For example, it is not necessary that they witness the death of their pet and the visit to cousins will only take place in the future. Nevertheless, such reported situations can have an emotional impact on children, given their capacity to mentally represent what they are told together with its emotional implications.

Last but not least, as they get older, children will gradually come to share the collective representations and assumptions of the surrounding culture. They will typically accept the historical narratives, the sense of group identity well as the religious beliefs, of those around them. Those shared realities, and the commitments that they imply, will influence when they feel pride, sadness, relief and anger. No matter whether the emotionally charged event is a soccer match, the death of a princess, the desecration of a building or statue, or the election of a leader, the sense of belonging to an imagined community (Anderson, 2006) will increasingly shape children's emotional reactions, as they get older.

Conclusions

The psychological study of emotion was initiated during an era when evolutionary theorizing, and the continuities between man and animals, guided and inspired the scientific imagination. This is evident if we look back at the early writings of Darwin, James and Sully and at the subsequent twentieth century contributions of Ekman and Bowlby. In their own individual ways, they subscribed to a strongly ethological view in which an emotion was to be conceived as a set of facial, bodily, and indeed neural reactions to an ongoing or imminent situation, and typically a situation with some biological significance for the individual facing it. Hence, the focus on the fear experienced by an adult at the approach of a bear or on the distress experienced by an infant at the departure of an attachment figure. Implicit in this approach to emotion is a diachronic element, but the time frame is that of 'big history' – of evolutionary change and continuity across scores of millennia. The shorter time frame of human history rarely plays a role in this approach even if there are occasional allusions by all three of the nineteenth century authors to the differences between civilization and savagery.

My own sense is that psychological and historical research would benefit from the recognition that human emotions are indeed like those of other animals, especially those of non-human primates, but that there are also deep differences alongside those similarities. The differences that I have focused on are all ultimately linked to the fact that human evolution ventured into, and made a success of, a highly distinctive mode of survival – one that is based on the cross-generational transmission of culture-specific practices rather than species-wide strategies. That cross-generational transmission presupposes that children are receptive to local practices, beliefs and loyalties. They must, as I have argued elsewhere, be gifted anthropologists who, without at first knowing the local language or the surrounding culture, have the capacities to figure them out and to become an acculturated member (Harris, 2012b). The implications of this view are steadily being worked out with respect to cognitive development. The portrait of the child as a thoughtful and relatively autonomous scientist who is mainly engaged in hands-on investigation of the natural world – a portrait that dominated a great deal of research in cognitive development during the 2nd half of the twentieth century – is gradually being augmented by recognition of children's cognitive skill in navigating, understanding, and re-enacting the cultural practices that surround them (Goodnow, Miller, & Kessel, 1995; Rogoff, 2003).

However, this 'new look' in the study of cognitive development has not had much impact on the study of emotional development. There, we continue to see echoes of James's claim that emotions, especially in children, are a set of prepared neural reactions to ongoing encounters with the world's primordial furniture – its threats, challenges and benefactions. In this essay, I have tried to underline aspects of emotional development that would imply a much greater role for culture – and for historical change – than the Jamesian account would underwrite. First, I have emphasized that even in navigating the natural world, children consult other people for emotional guidance. Second, thanks to their language ability, children can express not just their current feelings – they can also report on past and future feelings. Indeed, in dialogue with a caregiver or a clinician, they can talk or write about earlier emotionally charged episodes, recall, and sometimes re-appraise, what they felt and why they did so. Third, because of their imagination, children can be moved by the reports of a situation rather than a direct encounter. Finally, as they get older, the situations that elicit children's various emotional reactions consist increasingly of phenomena that derive their emotional significance from the meaning given them by the surrounding culture rather than from any implications that they might have for biological survival.

Disclosure statement

No potential conflict of interest was reported by the author.

References

Alexander, K. J., Miller, P. J., & Hengst, J. A. (2001). Young children's emotional attachments to stories. *Social Development, 10*, 374–398. doi:10.1111/1467-9507.00171

Anderson, B. (2006). *Imagined communities*. London: Verso.

Barrett, L. F. (2011). Was Darwin wrong about emotional expressions? *Current Directions in Psychological Science, 20*, 400–406. doi:10.1177/0963721411429125

Bowlby, J. (1973). *Attachment and loss, vol. 2: Separation, anxiety and anger*. London: The Hogarth Press.

Cheney, D. L., & Seyfarth, R. M. (1992). *How monkeys see the world: Inside the mind of another species*. Chicago, IL: Chicago University Press.

Darwin, C. (1872). *The expression of the emotions in man and animals*. London: John Murray.

Darwin, C. (1877). A biographical sketch of an infant. *Mind, 2*, 285–294.

De Wolff, M., & van IJzendoorn, M. H. (1997). Sensitivity and attachment: A meta-analysis on parental antecedents of infant attachment. *Child Development, 68*, 571–591. doi:10.2307/1132107

Ekman, P. (1973). Cross-cultural studies of facial expression. In P. Ekman (Ed.), *Darwin and facial expression* (pp. 169–222). New York, NY: Academic Press.

Ekman, P., & Darwin, C. (2009). *The expression of the emotions in man and animals*. Oxford: Oxford University Press.

Ekman, P., & Friesen, W. (1971). Constants across cultures in the face and emotion. *Journal of Personality and Social Psychology, 17*, 124–129. doi:10.1037/h0030377

Gibson, E., & Walk, R. D. (1960). The 'visual cliff'. *Scientific American, 202*, 64–71. doi:10.1038/scientificamerican0460-64

Goodnow, J. J., Miller, P. J., & Kessel, F. (1995). *Cultural practices as contexts for development*. San Francisco, CA: Jossey-Bass.

Harris, P. L. (2000). *The work of the imagination*. Oxford: Blackwell.

Harris, P. L. (2012a). *Trusting what you're told: How children learn from others*. Cambridge, MA: The Belknap Press/Harvard University Press.

Harris, P. L. (2012b). The child as anthropologist. *Infancia y Aprendizaje, 35*, 276–277. doi:10.1174/021037012802238920

Harris, P. L. (2016). Missing persons. In J. Dodd (Ed.), *Art, mind, and narrative: Themes from the work of Peter Goldie* (pp. 190–206). Oxford: Oxford University Press.

Henrich, J. (2015). *The secret of our success: How culture is driving human evolution, domesticating our species, and making us smarter*. Princeton, NJ: Princeton University Press.

Herrmann, E., Call, J., Hernandez-Lloreda, M. V., Hare, B., & Tomasello, M. (2007). Humans have evolved specialized skills of social cognition: The Cultural intelligence hypothesis. *Science, 317*, 1360–1366. doi:10.1126/science.1146282

Hornik, R., Risenhoover, N., & Gunnar, M. (1987). The effects of maternal positive, neutral, and negative affective communications on infant responses to new toys. *Child Development, 58*, 937–944. doi:10.2307/1130534

Hrdy, S. B. (2009). *Mothers and others*. Cambridge, MA: Belknap Press/Harvard University Press.

James, W. (1884). What is an emotion? *Mind, 9*, 188–205.

Lewis, M. (2014). *The rise of consciousness and the development of emotional life*. New York, NY: The Guilford press.

Liberman, Z., Woodward, A. L., Sullivan, K. R., & Kinzler, K. D. (2016). Early emerging system for reasoning about the social nature of foods. *PNAS, 113*, 9480–9485. doi:10.1073/pnas.1605456113

Nelson, C. A., Fox, N. A., & Zeanah, C. H. (2014). *Romania's abandoned children: Deprivation, brain development, and the struggle for recovery*. Cambridge, MA: Harvard University Press.

Passman, R. H., & Longeway, K. P. (1982). The role of vision in maternal attachment: Giving 2-year-olds a photograph of their mother during separation. *Developmental Psychology, 18*, 530–533. doi:10.1037/0012-1649.18.4.530

Richerson, P. J., & Boyd, R. (2005). *Not by genes alone: How culture transformed human evolution*. Chicago, IL: Chicago University Press.

Robertson, J., & Robertson, J. (1971). Young children in brief separation: A fresh look. *The Psychoanalytic Study of the Child, 26*, 264–315.

Rogoff, B. (2003). *The cultural nature of human development*. New York, NY: Oxford University Press.

Russell, J. A. (1994). Is there universal recognition of emotion from facial expression? A review of the cross-cultural studies. *Psychological Bulletin, 115*, 102–141. doi:10.1037/0033-2909.115.1.102

Rutter, M., Colvert, E., Kreppner, J., Beckett, C., Castle, J., Groothues, C., … Sonuga-Barke, E. J .S. (2007). Early adolescent outcomes for institutionally deprived and non-deprived adoptees. I: Disinhibited attachment. *Journal of Child Psychology and Psychiatry, 48*, 17–30. doi:10.1111/j.1469-7610.2006.01688.x

Schwartz, A. N., Campos, J. J., & Baisel, E. J. (1973). The visual cliff: Cardiac and behavioral responses on the deep and shallow sides at five and nine months of age. *Journal of Experimental Child Psychology, 15*, 86–99. doi:10.1016/0022-0965(73)90133-1

Shuttleworth, S. S. (2013). *The mind of the child: Child development in literature, science, and medicine 1840–1900*. Oxford: Oxford University Press.

Shutts, K., Kinzler, K. D., & DeJesus, J. M. (2013). Understanding infants' and children's social learning about foods: Previous research and new prospects. *Developmental Psychology, 40*, 419–425. doi:10.1037/0012-1649.44.3.734

Sorce, J. F., Emde, R. N., Campos, J. J., & Klinnert, M. D. (1985). Maternal emotional signaling: Its effect on the visual cliff behavior of 1-year-olds. *Developmental Psychology, 21*, 195–200. doi:10.1037/0012-1649.21.1.195

Stenberg, G. (2013). Do 12-month-old infants trust a competent adult? *Infancy, 18*, 873–904. doi:10.1111/infa.12011

Sully, J. (1918). *My life and friends: A psychologist's memories*. London: T. Fisher Unwin.

Tamis-LeMonda, C. S., Adolph, K. E., Lobo, S. A., Karasik, L. B., Ishak, S., & Dimitropoulou, K. A. (2008). When infants take mothers' advice: 18-month-olds integrate perceptual and social information to guide motor action. *Developmental Psychology, 44*, 734–746. doi:10.1037/0012-1649.44.3.734

Taylor, M. (1998). *Imaginary companions and the children who create them*. New York, NY: Oxford University Press.

Wellman, H. M., Harris, P. L., Banerjee, M., & Sinclair, A. (1995). Early understanding of emotion: Evidence from natural language. *Cognition and Emotion, 9*, 117–149. doi:10.1080/02699939508409005

Putting attachment in its place: Disciplinary and cultural contexts

Marga Vicedo

ABSTRACT
This paper examines the reception of John Bowlby's and Mary Ainsworth's ethological theory of attachment among anthropologists and cultural psychologists. First, it shows that from Margaret Mead's criticisms in the mid 1950s to the present, many of them have challenged the main tenets of attachment theory but attachment theorists ignored those challenges. Second, it argues that we need to understand the different disciplinary goals of psychology and anthropology after WWII in order to illuminate the lack of attention to children's cultural context in attachment research. The privileging within psychology of laboratory data over field observations supported the rise of attachment research focused on the strange situation procedure and contributed to the neglect of ethnographic data about children in their socio-cultural milieu. Recognizing the importance of studying children in context, however, recent studies by anthropologists and developmental psychologists sensitive to the power of culture have deepened the challenge to attachment theory.

Introduction

In 1951 British psychiatrist John Bowlby published a widely influential report, *Maternal Care and Mental Health*, for the World Health Organization. He asserted that psychiatrists and psychologists had determined that maternal care and love is essential for the proper emotional development of infants (Bowlby, 1951). In the following years, Bowlby turned to animal studies to develop his ethological attachment theory. According to this theory, evolution has designed a system of attachment between mother and child; without that secure attachment, children grow up emotionally scarred (Bowlby, 1969). Since American/Canadian psychologist Mary Ainsworth presented empirical work to support Bowlby's views, today they are considered the co-founders of the ethological attachment theory, which has become an influential paradigm in child-socialization.

Yet, numerous critics have pointed out substantial flaws in attachment theory. My historical examination of the development and reception of Bowlby's and Ainsworth's views from the 1950s to the 1980s showed that they ignored the criticisms (Vicedo, 2013). In this book, I focused on Bowlby's appeal to animal research in order to support his theory.

Here, I want to show how many anthropologists and cultural psychologists have also challenged attachment theory from its inception. First, I present Margaret Mead's views. Mead noted that her own studies in non-Western societies revealed the existence of a greater diversity of behavior than Bowlby's theory acknowledged. However, Bowlby and Ainsworth ignored the call to recognize the diversity of child rearing patterns uncovered by ethnographic studies. Second, I analyze how the strange situation, a laboratory procedure to evaluate attachment patterns developed by Ainsworth, contributed to the success of attachment theory. I argue that the rise of attachment theory, despite the glaring omission of data about a variety of cultures, was enabled in part by the focus of psychologists on laboratory procedures. This methodological preference contributed to the study of children in isolation from their socio-cultural contexts. Nevertheless, from the 1980s on, ethnographic work about mothers, children, and families in their socio-cultural contexts has deepened the challenges to central tenets of the ethological theory of attachment behavior and to the primacy of the laboratory over fieldwork in studies of human behavior and emotions.

Mead: Variability in the field

Margaret Mead was among the first anthropologists who paid serious attention to childhood in her work about Samoan society and her photographic study of children in Balinese culture (Bateson & Mead, 1942). She became one of the leaders of the Culture and Personality movement, which aimed to study the effects of childrearing on individual personality and larger social structures. With the rise of interest in children's emotional development after WWII, Mead became a prominent participant in interdisciplinary discussions about this topic.

Mead expressed her concern about growing trends in child development research around mid-century. Commenting on Bowlby's (1951) WHO report and other studies that also emphasized the detrimental effects of maternal separation, she deplored the inflated statements about the role of a single factor in child rearing and the 'exaggerated and poorly supported claims of the importance of the mother as a single figure in the infant's life' (Mead, 1954, p. 476). Contrary to Bowlby and other researchers who focused almost exclusively on the role of mothers, Mead maintained that 'the character formation of the child represents the child's total environmental situation as it is responded to and introcepted by that child in terms of its constitution and individual life history' (Mead, 1954, p. 474). In her opinion, many authors overstated the damaging effects on children of separation – even for brief times – from their mothers. Mead pointed out that there was no anthropological evidence to support 'the value of such an accentuation of *the tie between mother and child*. On the contrary, cross-cultural studies suggest that adjustment is most facilitated if the child is cared for by many warm, friendly people' (Mead, 1954, p. 477, my emphasis). Bowlby, however, continued to focus on the tie between mother and child.

Ignoring Mead's criticisms, Bowlby tellingly entitled his first presentation of his ethological theory of attachment, 'The nature of the child's tie to his mother.' In this classic paper, Bowlby did not review data from different cultures. Nevertheless, he postulated a biological basis for the bond between a mother and her child and argued that a secure bond is necessary for a child's adequate psychological development (Bowlby, 1958). However, many scholars criticized the data Bowlby was relying upon, and in 1962 the WHO published a reassessment of its 1951 report (WHO, 1962). Although this publication is rarely cited, in contrast to the 1951 WHO report this volume included articles by major researchers who criticized the conclusions Bowlby drew from existing studies about maternal separation. Among many methodological flaws that they criticized were his extrapolations from studies about maternal deprivation in extreme circumstances to the everyday relations between mothers and children in regular households. Bowlby declined an opportunity to reply to his critics. But he supervised the reply offered by Ainsworth in this volume (see Vicedo, 2013 for further details).

Mead penned one of papers in that 1962 volume, and again pointed out the existence of different types of families and child rearing practices. In her view, Bowlby wrongly assumed that childcare could 'not be safely distributed among several figures,' and that all separations from mother were 'necessarily harmful in character, emotionally damaging, if not completely lethal' (Mead, 1962, p. 55). Mead claimed that studies of other cultures, including her own work in Samoa, showed that children who were cared for by different people grew up to be well-adjusted individuals. She concluded that by giving the mores of his own culture the status of universal behavior and positing a biological underpinning, Bowlby had committed the sin of 'reification' (Mead, 1962, p. 58).

Mead and other anthropologists in this period emphasized the need to conduct further cross-cultural and interdisciplinary studies before making any assertions about the universality of behavior and emotions. Those studies showed an enormous diversity of practices and beliefs about childrearing in diverse societies (Mead, 1954, 1955; Whiting & Child, 1953; on culture and personality studies, see Levine, 2001).

In contrast, Bowlby appealed to studies of animal behavior to support his views. Building upon his 1958 paper, in his influential 1969 book *Attachment* he claimed that the attachment between mother and child is an adaptation forged by natural selection in the ancestral environment of human evolution. Further, deviations from the mother-child patterns already set in that environment would lead to child pathologies and imperil human survival. Again, although he postulated a theory of child development of universal character, Bowlby did not review the existing ethnographic literature on children. He mentioned Mead only once in a footnote, just to state briefly she had misunderstood him (Bowlby, 1969, p. 303). However, he offered no explanation or rebuttal of her arguments.

Bowlby's reliance on animal studies (the work of Konrad Lorenz, Niko Tinbergen, and Harry Harlow) and his claim that attachment was an adaptation became central to the success of his ethological theory of attachment. First, his book came out during a period of unprecedented interest in animal behavior during the late 1960s and 1970s; as evidence suffice it to note that Lorenz and Tinbergen won the Nobel Prize in Physiology and Medicine in 1973. Second, by appealing to the higher authority of biology Bowlby's views on attachment benefitted from a halo effect. However, I have argued elsewhere that Bowlby selectively referred to those studies supporting his positions while ignoring other studies that did not support his views (Vicedo, 2013; for a critical rebuttal of attachment theorists' appeal to evolution and animal studies, see Vicedo, 2017a). Yet, as important as Bowlby's appeal to biology was, it is doubtful that his theory would have become widespread were it not for the development of a laboratory tool that allowed attachment researchers to operationalize the study of attachment relations. American/Canadian psychologist Mary Ainsworth carried out the work that according to attachment scholars provided the empirical support for Bowlby's theory.

Ainsworth: Uniformity in the laboratory

During 1954–1955, Ainsworth studied infant care practices among the Ganda people of central Africa. For a period of 7 months, she conducted home visits to about 20 Ugandan households to observe the interaction between mothers and 28 infants. After moving to Johns Hopkins University in the United States in 1955, Ainsworth conducted another observational study of 26 White, middle-class mother-infant pairs in Baltimore.

Neither of these studies included in-depth ethnographic information about the socio-economic or cultural context of the families and about their goals and beliefs about childrearing. Ainsworth's aim was not to understand childrearing practices in their socio-cultural context. Consonant with the psychological tradition in which she was trained and the universal aspirations of attachment theory, she aimed to discover universal patterns of behavior and their causes.

In 1967 Ainsworth published *Infancy in Uganda*. To assess attachment, she focused on three aspects of an infant's behavior: the use of mother as a secure base for exploration; the infant's distress during brief separations from mother;

and the infant's fear when encountering strangers. She classified the infants she had observed in three groups: secure-attached, insecure-attached, and non-attached. Ainsworth identified several factors as significant for the development of infant-mother attachment, but she concluded that the determinant ones were the conduct and the feelings of the mother, mainly her sensitivity in responding to her baby's signals (Ainsworth, 1967, p. 400).

In the Baltimore home study, Ainsworth could not observe the attachment behaviors she had identified in her Ugandan study. But Ainsworth did not see those negative results as evidence for the diversity of children's behaviors in different cultures. Rather than interpreting those observations as a challenge to the universality of attachment responses, she devised a procedure to try to elicit the behaviors she had observed in Uganda: the Strange Situation Procedure (SSP). This 20-min laboratory experiment comprised 7 episodes of 3 min each. Twenty-three of the infants from the Baltimore study, ranging in age from 9 to 24 months, were tested to see how they reacted when their mothers left them in an unfamiliar environment alone, with a stranger, and also how they responded upon being reunited with their mothers.

The alleged power of the SSP grew quickly. In a short period, researchers went from presenting it as a tool used to elicit children's behaviors to accepting it as a reliable test used to categorize infants. They moved from justifying its use as a hypothesis-generating procedure to claiming that it was a method capable of establishing causal relations. In 1970 Ainsworth and Bell (1970, p. 52) put forward the SSP as a tool 'to illustrate' children's attachment and exploratory behaviors in a 'laboratory microcosm.' But in 1978 Ainsworth, Blehar, Waters, and Wall (1978) presented the SSP as a reliable test for categorizing not only behaviors, but also children and their mothers. Depending mainly on the infant's behavior upon the mother's return, the infants were classified as securely attached, anxious-avoidant, and anxious-resistant (1978, p. xi). Since the authors claimed that maternal sensitivity is the main factor shaping the attachment, the categorization of children automatically entailed a categorization of the mothers as well. As they put it:

> ... the findings here reported suggest that one can establish a fair basis for predicting strange-situation behavior from home behavior and, perhaps more important, that one can assess certain general aspects of the infant's characteristic relationship with his mother from his behavior in the strange situation. (Ainsworth et al., 1978, p. 135)

Thus, according to these attachment theorists, a twenty-minute laboratory procedure sufficed to establish causal relations between a mother's care and her child's personality. Furthermore, Ainsworth et al. argued that their findings were normative and supported Bowlby's theory of attachment (Ainsworth et al., 1978, p. 95).

In my view, the SSP procedure played a crucial part in the advancement of Bowlby's theory among American researchers because it fitted well within the dominant *vision of science* that psychologists defended. Psychology is a large field that embraces many different approaches. But, as historians of science have documented (Herman, 1995; Solovey, 2013), after WWII a large number of psychologists and social scientists increasingly turned towards a model of science that aimed to emulate the natural sciences in their reliance on experiments, predictions, and universal generalizations. Developmental psychologists critical of triumphalist narratives of their field have also noted this scientistic turn. Moving away from its interdisciplinary beginnings, child development studies focused increasingly on psychology and on 'one conception of that discipline – as an experimental laboratory endeavor seeking universal generalizations and principles along the lines of the physical and biological sciences,' as Kessel (2009, p. 830) noted.

In addition, attachment theory supported a particular *vision of children* that gained currency after WWII. Mayes and Lassonde (2014, p. 6) have identified several defining features in the American postwar developmental paradigm, including 'a declining faith in children's innate resiliency and preprogrammed constitutional strength in favor of a view of children as fragile and highly sensitive to their environments; a scheme of children's development as stage-like with consequential outcomes,' and the stress on 'the influence of parental care.' For Bowlby and Ainsworth, a secure attachment between mother and child has to develop early on in order for emotional development to proceed in the right way. They also saw children as possessing no resilience to overcome the lack of sensitive parenting. Thus, their views about infants and about the significance or parental care fitted well within the postwar developmental paradigm.

However, towards the end of the 1970s, several prominent child psychologists criticized the vision of science and of children supported by attachment theory as atomistic and reductionistic. In direct reference to SSP studies, Urie Bronfenbrenner (1977, p. 513) minced no words: 'Much of contemporary developmental psychology is the science of the strange behavior of children in strange situations with strange adults for the briefest possible periods of time.' In 'The American child and other cultural inventions' William Kessen criticized the universalistic aspirations of contemporary developmental psychology by calling attention to the different conceptions of childhood and of science existing in different times and places. Kessen found especially problematic the belief in a 'free standing' and 'self-contained' child with its instincts, traits, and attachments as essential components of its nature. Not only was it empirically incorrect, but that vision also enabled psychologists to take the child as the unit of study rather than considering the child as part of a more complex system of relations and network of influences. Thus, the conception of the 'isolable' child had important and troubling methodological consequences: 'Basically, we have observed those parts of development that the child could readily transport to our laboratories or to our testing sites' (Kessen, 1979, p. 819). In sum, critical voices pointed out that the reliance on laboratory experiments led developmental psychologists to a distorted vision of children because it ignored the role of context in child development.

The need to study children in context became a recurrent theme in discussions about the state of developmental psychology. In the 1979 special issue of *American Psychologist* that the APA dedicated to 'Psychology and Children' Brofenbrenner pointed to the 'missing data' on contexts of child reading in studies of human development, and called for explorations of how ecological contexts affect the course of psychological growth (Bronfenbrenner, 1979, p. 844). Michael Cole and his collaborators at the Laboratory of Comparative Human Cognition at UC-San Diego criticized developmental research that did not acknowledge what anthropologist Franz Boas had stated as early as 1911: 'The existence of a mind absolutely independent of conditions of life is unthinkable.' They argued that taking this insight seriously 'would entail recognizing that laboratory tasks cannot stand alone as a privileged means for discovering psychological principles.' And they concluded: 'Cross-cultural psychology has forced upon us the recognition that interplay between laboratory and observational research is a necessity if we are to understand how experience affects our minds' (LCHC, 1979, pp. 829, 832). Schwartz wrote that developmental psychology had 'largely missed the opportunity to consider the child in the cultural milieu, which is the sine qua non of the developmental completion of a human nature' (1981, pp. 11, 12). Super and Harkness (1986) also criticized the focus on the universal and decontextualized child and put forward the concept of the 'developmental niche' to include an individual's experience of culture and environmental influences.

Despite the fact that these and other researchers from anthropology and cultural psychology continued to call for a better integration of ethnographic insights obtained in the field with the knowledge gained via experimental and observational studies in the lab, some researchers remained pessimistic. Gustav Jahoda lamented that, despite the rise of cross-cultural developmental studies, developmental psychology remained 'unduly parochial' because major areas were not taking cultural diversity seriously (Jahoda, 1986, p. 417). Still, he saw the cross-cultural study of emotional development as a promising and exciting field. The cross-cultural study of the emotions would indeed blossom in the late 1980s. But this rich work on diverse communities and time periods did not become integrated with attachment research.

Most attachment researchers continued to focus on using the SSP procedure to study children in the lab, despite the challenges mentioned above to this approach as well as the mounting critiques to the procedure itself. In the mid-eighties, several researchers disputed the SSP's validity and reliability in the Baltimore study (Kagan, 1984; Lamb et al., 1984). In addition, other scholars have pointed out that the SSP embeds Western cultural assumptions and thus cannot be used to study children in non-Western cultures (Levine & Miller, 1990; Meehan & Hawks, 2013; Rothbaum, Weisz, Pott, Miyke, & Morelli, 2000; see also

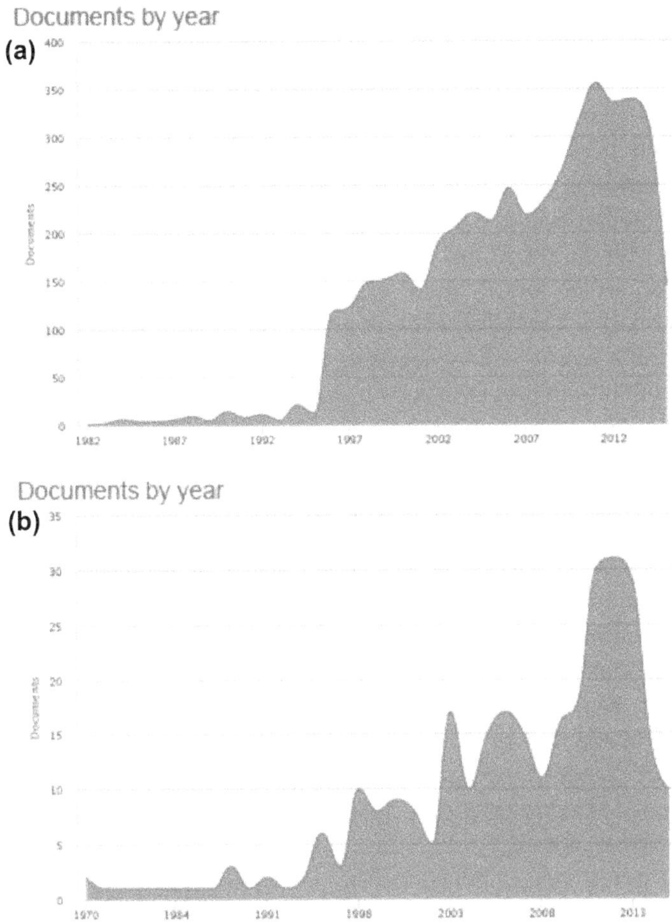

Figure 1. (a) Publications citing *Patterns of Attachment* (1978) (from Scopus), (b) Publications citing *Infancy in Uganda* (1967) (from Scopus).

Vicedo, 2013 for a critique of the view that the SSP results provide evidence for Bowlby's views).

Yet, the SSP's ability to operationalize research on attachment facilitated an explosion of work. To put it plainly, administering a 20-min test in the confines of a laboratory is a much easier, faster, and cheaper method to obtain fast results and publications than conducting a field ethnographic study away from your own home and office. A comparison of citations of Ainsworth's books, *Patterns of Attachment* and *Infancy in Uganda* illustrates the prominence of the SSP, and shows how the laboratory instrument achieved far greater prominence than her observational study. *Patterns of Attachment* (Figure 1(a)) has been cited between ten and fifteen times more often than *Infancy in Uganda* (Figure 1(b)).

It is worth pointing out the irony in attachment researchers' reliance on the SSP procedure while ignoring observational studies of children in different contexts. Bowlby and Ainsworth emphasized their ethological approach in all their writings. However, ethologists Konrad Lorenz and Niko Tinbergen had made observation in natural environments the rallying call of their new approach to study behavior in an objective manner. As a corollary, ethologists sharply criticized the behaviorists' analysis of animal behavior in the laboratory. For them, the artificial conditions of the laboratory distorted the natural behavior of animals. Furthermore, for them, experiments were always secondary to field observation. One had to first observe animals in their ecological context. Only after having a thorough knowledge of an animal's behavioral patterns in his natural habitat should an ethologist turn to laboratory or experimental studies. Indeed, Tinbergen privately expressed his shock upon discovering that Bowlby had not carried out observational studies of children in order to develop his views about child development (Vicedo, 2017b).

Contrary to the ethological approach in which context is integral to understanding behavior, the bulk of attachment research has relied on the SSP, a cheap, quick, and simple laboratory procedure, has focused on testing a single variable (security), and has appealed to a single explanatory factor (maternal sensitivity). Mead's fears that child development research often isolated one single factor and that factor was usually the mother have remained pertinent in the field of attachment.

In recent decades, however, anthropologists have challenged the universalistic claims of attachment theory again on the basis of extensive research on diverse cultural settings.

Anthropology re-dux: Infants and mothers in context

A full account of ethnographic studies of childhood is beyond the scope of this paper. But a brief overview of some recent work about mothers and children reveals how the diversity uncovered calls into question basic tenets of attachment theory.

In an influential study, *Death Without Weeping,* Nancy Scheper-Hughes showed how the socio-economic context influences maternal attitudes and emotions. She followed three generations of mothers living in the slums of Brazil where the average woman had 9.5 pregnancies, 8 births, and 3.5 infant deaths. Aware that their babies may not survive, the mothers did not immediately 'personalize' their infants, did not name them right after birth, and did not mourn their deaths as is common in Western culture. Scheper-Hughes concluded that mother love is not a uniform, universal, and naturally monolithic affect. Challenging attachment theory, she called for recognizing that mother love 'represents a matrix of images, meanings, sentiments, and practices that are everywhere socially and culturally produced' (Scheper-Hughes, 1992, p. 341; see also Scheper-Hughes, 2014).

Other anthropologists demonstrated that socio-cultural contexts influence parents' goals in childrearing and, consequently, their practices, including their emotional involvement with their infants. Levine et al. (1994) found that Kenyan Gusii mothers, who bear an average of 10 children, focus first on their survival and then on teaching them compliance, contrary to mothers in the U.S. who do not aim for compliance in childrearing. In her studies of Samoan family relations, Mageo (2013) found that socialization is not oriented to develop feelings of security, but to encourage separation. Since mothers have diverse goals depending on their socio-economic conditions, cultural traditions, and social class, they also assess children's behavior differently. For example, Harwood, Miller, and Irizarry (1995) discovered that U.S. mothers in the Anglo and Puerto Rican communities of Connecticut have different conceptions of what a 'good child' is, and these affected their assessment of their children's behavior in a simulated strange situation. Some mothers disapproved of 'secure' behavior and approved of behavior that would be classified as 'insecure.' Weisner (2005) also reported that some U.S. mothers were happy to see their child behave in an 'independent' way, though that behavior corresponded to the 'avoidant' category in the attachment classification system. Thus, even in middle-class US groups, parents may not desire the behavior that attachment scholars consider both natural and ideal.

Cross-cultural studies have also made clear that, contrary to attachment theory's focus on the mother-infant dyad, childrearing is often a cooperative enterprise. As Mead pointed out in her criticisms of Bowlby's views in the mid-fifties, distributed care is quite common. In many societies, mothers are not the only ones taking care of children: siblings, fathers, aunts, grandparents, and other members of the community are involved in different ways. Developmental psychology has been slow in acknowledging this fact and its significance. Weisner and Gallimore (1977) pointed out that the 1969 *Handbook of Socialization Theory and Research* included practically no one but parents as caretakers in its 1182 pages. However, their review of anthropological studies showed the importance of children as caretakers of their siblings. More recent ethnographic work has confirmed that children and other family and community members are an intrinsic part of caretaking networks in many societies. Among the Beng people of West Africa, for example, a mother returns to work in the fields when her child is between 2 and 4 months old. During most of the day, diverse sitters carry the baby on their back from 5 to 20 min at a time. The comings and goings of children among caretakers are not perceived as a risk; on the contrary, they convey a feeling of safety to children (Gottlieb, 2004). For other studies of societies with distributive care (see Keller & Chaudhary, 2017; Meehan & Hawks, 2013; Morelli et al., 2017; Rogoff, 2003; Seymor, 2013; Weisner, 2014).

Finally, contrary to what attachment theory considers normative, parents in many communities try to avoid attaching to their infants right away. For example, in *The afterlife is where we come from: The culture of infancy in West Africa*, anthropologist Alma Gottlieb reports that some Beng mothers intentionally break the gaze of their infants to their own eyes in order to decrease their children's emotional attachment to them (Gottlieb, 2004, p. 161). Anthropologist David Lancy reviewed over 200 ethnographic and archaeological records from a variety of geographical areas and historical periods and found that in many societies infants are not given status as persons at birth and parents resist attaching to them. He concluded that these findings contradict the universal claims of attachment theorists (Lancy, 2015). In his view:

> 'Attachment theory' and its descendants have created a narrative of infants 'at risk' of emotional maladjustment. In this survey of sources from cultural anthropology, history, and archeology this perceived risk is absent … . The survey also reveals that an alternate narrative identifies attachment rather than attachment failure as the risk. A strong, emotional bond is seen as impeding a process whereby infants are pragmatically sorted into categories of wanted versus unwanted, timely versus untimely, legitimate versus illegitimate, strong fighters versus sickly ghosts, and innocent versus demonized, leading to sustained nurturance or extinction. (Lancy, 2014, p. 89)

Clearly, if mothers have a biological instinct for attachment, as Bowlby claimed, this innate impulse has been overridden by cultural beliefs and practices in these communities that delay forming emotional bonds with infants until their status is evaluated.

Furthermore, all these studies show that infants can thrive in a number of different environments and within diverse systems of child-care. As two more recent books also make clear (Gottlieb & DeLoache, 2016; Levine & Levine, 2016), children across the world are raised in many different ways. In many societies, multiple care is a widespread and normal practice.

In sum, ethnographic studies of child-rearing beliefs, goals, and practices in different societies have challenged the universalistic claims of attachment theory and its focus on the mother-infant dyad. In addition, regardless of the accuracy of any particular study or the validity of any specific insight, the anthropological work has made clear that context matters when studying child-rearing practices, child development, and emotions in human societies. To explain behavior and affects, researchers must understand the meanings they acquire within a particular culture. As both anthropological and historical works have shown, child rearing practices depend on conceptions of the self, personhood, and the social good that vary among different societies and that have changed over time (Koops, 2003; Morelli et al., 2017).

Conclusion

In this paper I have examined some powerful criticisms that anthropologists and cultural psychologists leveled against attachment theory from its inception to the present. From Mead to current researchers cross-cultural investigations have demonstrated the existence of various visions of children and development. As Levine and Norman have put it: 'there is a wider range of pathways to normal emotional development than has been imagined in attachment theory' (2008, p. 139). Anthropologists have revealed the variability and diversity in conceptions of childhood and practices of childcare by studying children in context. On the basis of that work, many researchers have criticized the failure of attachment theorists to take culture seriously (Gottlieb, 2014; Keller & Bard, 2017; Lancy, 2014; Levine, 2014; Morelli et al., 2017; Otto & Keller, 2014; Quinn & Mageo, 2013; Weisner, 2014).

By showing the need to study children in context, cross-cultural studies have also challenged psychologists' reliance on laboratory experiments as the primary methodological tool for uncovering universal behaviors and emotions. In the case of attachment theory, I have argued that the alleged uniformity of attachment behaviors was not discovered in the field but constructed in the laboratory in problematic ways. Based on studies of isolated children, attachment theorists postulated the existence of universal patterns of attachment. But children do not grow up in isolation. Thus, the evidence collected in the lab always needs to be assessed in relation to the observations collected in field studies.

If children's development needs to be understood in context, so does the development of a scientific theory. Here, I have argued that the rise of attachment studies owes much to the disciplinary goals of psychological research. Riding upon the coattails of the natural sciences, psychology after WWII aimed to develop universal laws of human behavior that could be tested in the laboratory. In that context, Ainsworth's strange situation procedure became instrumental in the growth of attachment theory, despite the numerous criticisms of its application and its interpretation. Anthropologists of childhood, in contrast, emphasized the need for ethnographic observational studies of childrearing practices in order to understand the diversity of human experiences.

For several decades scholars have noted that different visions of science created a rift between psychology and anthropology (Edgerton, 1974; Price-Williams, 1974; Super & Harkness, 1986). Tensions between the two fields continue to exist in the area of child development as a consequence of their different epistemological and methodological commitments. As long as mainstream psychology remains committed to a model focused on 'revealing universal laws about human experience, personality, social life, and subjectivity' (Herman, 1995, p. 12), it is hard to see how it can accept the claim that 'there is no one human psychology and no one pathway of development' (Keller, 2007, p. 270). In the recent past, however, many psychologists have also recognized the need to study children in their socio-cultural milieu, which requires careful analysis of social networks (Lewis, 2005) and cultural contexts (Cole, 1996). Others have emphasized the need for a new framework of 'developmental contextualism' to understand the complex and changing relations affecting children's development across the lifespan (Lamb, 2005, p. 110). More and more psychologists now believe that 'human development is a cultural process' (Rogoff, 2003, p. 3).

Yet, neither the extensive anthropological literature nor the critical psychological literature have been integrated within attachment research. Thus, the challenges reviewed here have not been answered.

But we must end on an optimistic note. Recently, there has been a growing concern that many claims about behavior have been based mostly on data obtained about people from WEIRD (Western, Educated, Industrialized, Rich, and Democratic) societies (Henrich, Heine, & Norenzayan, 2010). Historians have also been accumulating evidence that cultural practices of childrearing and the meaning of emotions have changed through time (Mintz, 2009; Stearns, 2003). If cultural psychologists and anthropologists are right that 'culture and psyche make each other up' (Shweder & Sullivan, 1993, p. 498), the joint efforts of psychologists, anthropologists, and historians will be necessary to illuminate the co-evolution of cultural contexts and children's development. As Mead stressed half a century ago, understanding childhood requires interdisciplinary, cross-cultural studies of children in context.

Disclosure statement

No potential conflict of interest was reported by the author.

References

Ainsworth, M. D. S. (1967). *Infancy in Uganda: Infant care and the growth of love*. Baltimore, MD: Johns Hopkins University Press.

Ainsworth, M. D. S., & Bell, S. M. (1970). Attachment, exploration, and separation: Illustrated by the behavior of one-year-olds in a strange situation. *Child Development, 41*, 49–67.

Ainsworth, M. D. S., Blehar, M. C., Waters, E., & Wall, S. (1978). *Patterns of attachment: A psychological study of the strange situation*. Hillsdale, NJ: Erlbaum.

Bateson, G., & Mead, M. (1942). *Balinese character: A photographic analysis*. New York: New York Academy of Sciences.

Bowlby, J. (1951). *Maternal care and mental health*. Geneva: World Health Organization.

Bowlby, J. (1958). The nature of the child's tie to his mother. *International Journal of Psychoanalysis, 39*, 350–373.

Bowlby, J. (1969). *Attachment and loss, Vol. 1: Attachment*. New York, NY: Basic Books.

Bronfenbrenner, U. (1977). Toward an experimental ecology of human development. *American Psychologist, 32*, 513–531.

Bronfenbrenner, U. (1979). Contexts of child rearing. Problems and prospects. *American Psychologist, 34*, 844–850.

Cole, M. (1996). *Cultural psychology: A once and future discipline*. Cambridge: Cambridge University Press.

Edgerton, R. B. (1974). Cross-cultural psychology and psychological anthropology: One paradigm or two? *Reviews in Anthropology, 1*, 52–65.

Gottlieb, A. (2004). *The afterlife is where we come from: The culture of infancy in West Africa*. Chicago, IL: The University of Chicago Press.
Gottlieb, A. (2014). Is it time to detach from attachment theory? Perspectives from the West African rain forest. In H. Otto & H. Keller (Eds.), *Different faces of attachment: Cultural variations on a universal human need* (pp. 187–214). Cambridge: Cambridge University Press.
Gottlieb, A., & DeLoache, J. (2016). *A world of babies: Imagined childcare guides for eight societies* (Updated ed.). Cambridge: Cambridge University Press.
Harwood, R. L., Miller, J. G., & Irizarry, N. L. (1995). *Culture and attachment: Perceptions of the child in context*. New York, NY: The Guilford Press.
Henrich, J., Heine, H. J., & Norenzayan, A. (2010). The weirdest people in the world. *The Behavioral and Brain Sciences, 33*, 61–83.
Herman, E. (1995). *The romance of American psychology: Political culture in the age of experts*. Berkeley: The University of California Press.
Jahoda, G. (1986). A cross-cultural perspective on developmental psychology. *International Journal of Behavioral Development, 9*, 417–437.
Kagan, J. (1984). *The nature of the child*. New York, NY: Basic Books.
Keller, H. (2007). *Cultures of infancy*. Mahwah, NJ: Erlbaum.
Keller, H., & Chaudhary, N. (2017). Is the mother essential for attachment? Models of care in different cultures. In H. Keller & K. A. Bard (Eds.), *Contextualizing attachment: The cultural nature of attachment*. Cambridge, MA: MIT Press.
Keller, H. & Bard, K. A. (Eds.). (2017). *Contextualizing attachment: The cultural nature of attachment*. Cambridge, MA: MIT Press.
Kessel, F. S. (2009). Research on child development: Historical perspectives. In R. A. Shweder, et al. (Eds.), *The child: An encyclopedic companion* (pp. 828–833). Chicago, IL: University of Chicago Press.
Kessen, W. (1979). The American child and other cultural inventions. *American Psychologist, 34*, 815–820.
Koops, W. (2003). Imaging childhood. In W. Koops & M. Zuckerman (Eds.), *Beyond the century of the child. Cultural history and developmental psychology* (pp. 1–18). Philadelphia: University of Pennsylvania Press.
Laboratory of Comparative Human Cognition. (1979). Cross-cultural psychology's challenges to our ideas of children and development. *American Psychologist, 34*, 827–833.
Lamb, M. E. (2005). Attachments, social networks, and developmental contexts. *Human Development, 48*, 108–112.
Lamb, M. E., Thompson, R. A., Gardner, W. P., Charnov, E. L., & Estes, D. (1984). Security of infantile attachment as assessed in the "strange situation": Its study and biological interpretation. *The Behavioral and Brain Sciences, 7*, 127–147.
Lancy, D. F. (2014). "Babies aren't persons": A survey of delayed personhood. In H. Otto & H. Keller (Eds.), *Different faces of attachment: Cultural variations on a universal human need* (pp. 66–109). Cambridge: Cambridge University Press.
Lancy, D. F. (2015). *The Anthropology of childhood. Cherubs, chattel, changelings* (2nd ed.). Cambridge: Cambridge University Press.
Levine, R. A. (2001). Culture and personality studies, 1918–1960: Myth and history. *Journal of Personality, 69*, 803–818.
Levine, R. A. (2014). Attachment theory as cultural ideology. In H. Otto & H. Keller (Eds.), *Different faces of attachment: Cultural variations on a universal human need* (pp. 50–65). Cambridge: Cambridge University Press.

Levine, R. A., Dixon, S., Levine, S., Richman, A., Leiderman, P. H., Keefer, C. H., & Brazelton, T. B. (1994). *Child care and culture: Lessons from Africa.* New York, NY: Cambridge University Press.

Levine, R. A., & Levine, S. (2016). *Do parents matter? Why Japanese babies sleep soundly, Mexican siblings don't fight, and American families should just relax.* New York, NY: PublicAffairs.

Levine, R. A., & Miller, P. M. (1990). Commentary. *Human Development, 33,* 73–80.

Levine, R. A., & Norman, K. (2008). Attachment in anthropological perspective. In R. A. Levine & R. S. New (Eds.), *Anthropology and child development: A cross-cultural reader* (pp. 127–142). Malden, MA: Wiley Blackwell.

Lewis, M. (2005). The child and its family: The social network model. *Human Development, 48,* 8–27.

Mageo, J. M. (2013). Toward a cultural psychodynamics of attachment: Samoa and US comparison. In N. Quinn & J. Mageo (Eds.), *Attachment reconsidered: Cultural perspectives on a Western theory* (pp. 191–214). New York, NY: Palgrave.

Mayes, L. C., & Lassonde, S. (2014). Introduction. In L. C. Mayes & S. Lassonde (Eds.), *A girl's childhood: Psychological development, social change, and the Yale child study center* (pp. 1–11). New Haven, CT: Yale University Press.

Mead, M. (1954). Some theoretical considerations on the problem of mother-child separation. *American Journal of Orthopsychiatry, 24,* 471–483.

Mead, M. (1955). Theoretical settings-1954. In M. Mead & M. Wolfenstein (Eds.), *Childhood in contemporary cultures* (pp. 3–20). Chicago, IL: The University of Chicago Press.

Mead, M. (1962). A cultural anthropologist's approach to maternal deprivation. *Deprivation of maternal care: A reassessment of its effects* (pp. 45–62). Geneva: World Health Organization.

Meehan, C. L., & Hawks, S. (2013). Cooperative breeding and attachment among the Aka foragers. In N. Quinn & J. Mageo (Eds.), *Attachment reconsidered: Cultural perspectives on a Western theory* (pp. 85–113). New York, NY: Palgrave.

Mintz, S. (2009). *Huck's raft: A history of American childhood.* Ann Arbor: University of Michigan.

Morelli, G. A., Chaudhary, N., Gottlieb, A., Keller, H., Murray, M., Quinn, N., Rosabal-Coto, M., Scheidecker, G., Takada, A., & Vicedo, M. (2017). Taking culture seriously: Developing a pluralistic theory of attachments. In H. Keller & K. A. Bard (Eds.), *Contextualizing attachment: The cultural nature of attachment.* Cambridge, MA: MIT Press.

Otto, H., & Keller, H. (Eds.). (2014). *Different faces of attachment: Cultural variations on a universal human need.* Cambridge: Cambridge University Press.

Price-Williams, D. (1974). Psychological experiment and anthropology: The problem of categories. *Ethos, 2,* 95–114.

Quinn, N., & Mageo, J. M. (Eds.). (2013). *Attachment reconsidered: Cultural perspectives on a western theory.* New York, NY: Palgrave Macmillan.

Rogoff, B. (2003). *The cultural nature of human development.* Oxford: Oxford University Press.

Rothbaum, F., Weisz, J., Pott, M., Miyke, K., & Morelli, G. (2000). Attachment and culture: Security in the United States and Japan. *American Psychologist, 55,* 1093–1104.

Scheper-Hughes, N. (1992). *Death without weeping: The violence of everyday life in Brazil.* Berkeley: University of California Press.

Scheper-Hughes, N. (2014). Family life as *bricolage* – reflections on intimacy and attachments in *Death without weeping*. In H. Otto & H. Keller (Eds.), *Different faces of attachment: Cultural variations on a universal human need* (pp. 230–260). Cambridge: Cambridge University Press.

Schwartz, T. (1981). The acquisition of culture. *Ethos, 9,* 4–17.

Seymor, S. C. (2013). "It takes a village to raise a child": Attachment theory and multiple child care in Alor, Indonesia, and in North India. In N. Quinn & J. M. Mageo (Eds.), *Attachment reconsidered: Cultural perspectives on a Western theory* (pp. 115–139). New York, NY: Palgrave Macmillan.

Shweder, R. A., & Sullivan, M. A. (1993). Cultural psychology: Who needs it? *Annual Review of Psychology, 44*, 497–523.

Solovey, M. (2013). *Shaky foundations: The politics-patronage-social science nexus in Cold War America*. New Brunswick, NJ: Rutgers University Press.

Stearns, P. N. (2003). *Anxious parents: A history of modern childrearing in America*. New York: New York University Press.

Super, C. M., & Harkness, S. (1986). The developmental niche: A conceptualization at the interface of child and culture. *International Journal of Behavioral Development, 9*, 545–569.

Vicedo, M. (2013). *The nature and nurture of love. From imprinting to attachment in Cold War America*. Chicago, IL: The University of Chicago Press.

Vicedo, M. (2017a). The strange situation of the ethological theory of attachment in historical perspective. In H. Keller & K. A. Bard (Eds.), *Contextualizing attachment: The cultural nature of attachment*. Cambridge, MA: MIT Press.

Vicedo, M. (2017b). Ethopathology and civilization diseases: Niko and Elisabeth Tinbergen on autism. *Canadian Bulletin of Medical History*.

Weisner, T. S. (2005). Attachment as a cultural and ecological problem with pluralistic solutions. *Human Development, 48*, 89–94.

Weisner, T. S. (2014). The socialization of trust: Plural caregiving and diverse pathways in human development across cultures. In H. Otto & H. Keller (Eds.), *Different faces of attachment: Cultural variations on a universal human need* (pp. 263–277). Cambridge: Cambridge University Press.

Weisner, T. S., & Gallimore, R. (1977). My brother's keeper: Child and sibling caretaking. *Current Anthropology, 18*, 169–190.

Whiting, J. W. M., & Child, I. L. (1953). *Child training and personality: A cross-cultural study*. New Haven, CT: Yale University Press.

World Health Organization. (1962). *Deprivation of maternal care: A reassessment of its effects*. Geneva: Author.

OPEN ACCESS

Attachment histories and futures: reply to Vicedo's 'Putting attachment in its place'

Robbie Duschinsky, Marinus Van Ijzendoorn, Sarah Foster, Sophie Reijman and Francesca Lionetti

For Vicedo, 'putting attachment in its place' seems to entail two aspects. The first is working to understand the rise of attachment theory and its place within the history of knowledge practices. The second is to criticize the validity of attachment theory. In this reply, we appraise three criticisms made by Vicedo of attachment theory, chosen as points for sustaining a dialogue. Our main point in this reply is that, in excluding the work of attachment researchers after Ainsworth from consideration, Vicedo's work is not yet able to properly 'put attachment in its place', in either sense of the phrase. At most, she puts Bowlby in the 1950s–1960s in his place, but without speaking effectively to subsequent attachment research. In our view, not just the validity, but the very meaning of attachment as a scientific research programme cannot be understood outside of its temporal context, and the relationship this entails between theory and research, past and future.

1. History and attachment research

In *The Nature and Nurture of Love*, Vicedo states that 'the scientific evidence in support of attachment theory has been insufficient and is deeply flawed' (2013, p. 238), a position that Vicedo continues to argue in 'Putting attachment in its place'. We agree that it is an appropriate part of the role of a historian of science to appraise the evidence under discussion. However, issues as well as insights may arise when a historian treats evidence of the contingent, social and messy origins of ideas as evidence of their lack of scientific validity. This is to miss the distinction, always relative but nonetheless often meaningful, between the generation of ideas and the slow nature of work to appraise their validity (cf. Schickore & Steinle, 2006). We fully acknowledge that most of Bowlby's ideas were not well-grounded in adequate supporting evidence, were influenced by contemporary ideologies, and that caution is needed in using those that have not seen adequate testing. This is often the case with the development of early theories across the sciences (Collins, 2004).

Furthermore, some of Bowlby's hypotheses have been very valuable, producing knowledge that is reliable and a good basis for the design of policies such as family rooming-in during a child's hospitalization. He was also right to contest the overemphasis on fantasy at the expense of the actuality of child experiences in the psychoanalytic thought of his day. He was absolutely right that child institutionalization is generally harmful and emotionally damaging (Dozier et al., 2014; Lionetti, Pastore, & Barone, 2015) although convincing empirical evidence was lacking 70 years ago (Bowlby, 1953). However, Bowlby was also wrong on many accounts, and Vicedo appropriately points to occasions where he expressed undue and unwarranted confidence in certain claims with potentially damaging social effects. One area where later research has rectified early theory has been in relation to daycare. Bowlby underestimated the role of child factors in the experience of daycare; researchers have found that infants with a prior tendency to be more readily upset appear to be more affected by the quality of care they experience – both negatively *and* positively – than other children (Pluess & Belsky, 2009). Bowlby's thinking also radically underspecified the concepts of 'separation' and 'deprivation'. As a consequence he was wrong that daycare is an experience of a similar kind as institutionalization, although his emphasis on continuity and sensitivity of care turned out empirically to be important factors for quality daycare. Longitudinal research following 1,153 children from infancy to adolescence found that quality day-care for young children whose mothers are highly stressed confers a net benefit (NICHD, 1997).

2. Continuities or discontinuities across generations of researchers

The tendency in Vicedo's writings to assume uncomplicated continuity from attachment research from the mid-1950s to the present has been criticized by both historians and psychologists. Midgley (2014, p. 266) describes Vicedo's account of attachment theory as 'polemical' since it seems to wish to debunk attachment research, but displays 'lack of attention to the work of Mary Main and others in the last forty years', and is therefore tellingly 'outdated', without purchase on the present (268). In her paper on 'Putting attachment in its place', as well as in her other work that we have seen, Vicedo excludes mention of subsequent developments in attachment theory by Ainsworth's students, or their students. Vicedo makes no mention of the cross-cultural work that attachment researchers have conducted. And she makes no citation of the field's journal *Attachment & Human Development* or the field's compendium, the *Handbook of Attachment* (now in its third edition; e.g. Mesman, van IJzendoorn, & Sagi-Schwartz, 2016). Other commentators have similarly observed that Vicedo's criticisms do not strike home because she conflates Bowlby with attachment theory and research, and underplays developments in Bowlby's thinking across time. Vicedo does not acknowledge that 'one can jettison the idea of mother love as instinctual, as well as the fixation on the mother as the crucial attachment figure, without discarding all of the theory's insights' (Plant, 2015, p. 459). The idea of mother love as instinctual was an early formulation especially to be found in Bowlby's *Child Care and the Growth of Love* (1953). Yet at least from 1964 (see PP/Bow/H.147), whilst there may be a short period where one or another caregiver is preferred when an infant is distressed, for Bowlby the attachment system was conceptualized as organized by the expectation that distributed caregiving may be available, and attachments made to various caregivers. Bowlby's last published work explicitly states the attachment system 'contributes to the individual's survival by keeping him or her in touch with one or more caregivers.' (1991, p. 306). Bowlby (1969, p. 303) wrote 'it has sometimes been alleged that I have expressed the view ... that mothering "cannot be safely distributed among several figures" (Mead, 1962). No such views have been expressed by me.' Vicedo's inclusion of Mead's allegation in 'Putting attachment in its place', but not Bowlby's direct reply to it, suggests partiality.

Later generations of attachment researchers have not held mother love to be instinctual, nor have they regarded it as necessary that the mother would be a child's sole attachment figure. The work of Sarah Hrdy (e.g. 2009) is an important contemporary influence in this regard. It is true, as Vicedo states, that siblings as caregivers have not yet received adequate attention in attachment research (but see the recent paper on infant–mother and infant–sibling attachment in Zambia by Mooya, Sichimba, & Bakermans-Kranenburg, 2016). For decades now, Bowlby's ideas have been elaborated in generating testable hypotheses on the development of attachment in social networks (e.g. Goossens & Ijzendoorn, 1990). In 'Putting attachment in its place' Vicedo states that the bulk of attachment research 'has focused on testing a single variable (security), and has appealed to a single explanatory factor (maternal sensitivity)' (692). However this has not been true for many decades as various meta-analyses document (e.g., Cyr, Euser, Bakermans-Kranenburg, & van Ijzendoorn, 2010). Nor was it inappropriate in the 1980s for this core hypothesis to have been a focus for a time, since extensive replication was needed in order to establish and, indeed, substantially qualify the standing of Ainsworth's empirical claims (Verhage et al., 2016).

3. The caregiving system

Another criticism of attachment research made by Vicedo which we feel has a certain purchase, but also limitations, are her claims relating to the conceptualization of caregiving. In *The Nature and Nurture of Love*, Vicedo states that 'In arguing that the mother is designed to fulfill her child's instinctual needs Bowlby transformed maternal love and care from a personal choice entailing devotion, work, patience, dedication, and not a few renunciations into a natural product of a woman's biological constitution' (2013, p. 90). In our assessment, this criticism holds well for Bowlby's popular writings of the 1950s. It does not hold quite so well for Bowlby's later thought, and it is a poor characterization of attachment research over the past decades. The adult caregiving behavioral system has been theorised as a construct conceptually and evolutionary distinct from the child attachment system, and as highly dependent on social support and cultural processes for whether, when and how they are deployed. And empirical operationalisations of the concept of caregiver sensitivity explicitly make space for situation-specific and child-related factors rather than prescribing concrete behaviors.

In 'Putting attachment in its place', Vicedo argues that 'contrary to what attachment theory considers normative, parents in many communities try to avoid attaching to their infants right away.' (2017, p. 693) Parental avoidance of emotional connection with their infant is certainly contrary to the normative picture of *Child Care and the Growth of Love*, and in the 1950s Bowlby sometimes, confusingly, used the term 'attachment' to refer to what he would later distinguish as the caregiving system. However, Vicedo's observation is in line with, not contrary to, attachment theory over the past decades. The idea that parents may use strategies to modulate the expression of caregiving behaviour, such as directing attention away from their child if they suspect that the child could be a source of distress, is well in line with the ideas of Mary Main and others at least from 1992. As well as theory, there has been empirical research exploring predictable individual differences regarding how children respond to cultural differences in caregiving sensitivity (Mesman et al., 2016). One relevant study that Vicedo may be interested to consider is Mesman et al. (2016b), who found significant differences in beliefs about the appropriateness of sensitive caregiving between cultural groups. Some of this effect was accounted for by group variations in poverty.

4. The validity of the ainsworth strange situation

A third set of criticisms made of attachment theory by Vicedo concerns the validity of the Strange Situation procedure. Vicedo argues that reliance on the Strange Situation has 'led developmental psychologists to a distorted vision of children because it ignored the role of context in child development.' (2017, p. 689). Again, Vicedo's claims have some relevance but are substantially outdated. It is true that too few attachment researchers include detailed ethnographic observations of naturalistic contexts when conducting their research, because there might be more to discover and grounded hypotheses to be developed. Nonetheless, there has been substantial study of children's social contexts and how these affect the development of their attachments (e.g., Cyr et al., 2010; Sroufe et al. 2005). Furthermore, infant behaviour in the Strange Situation has repeatedly been found to be associated with extensive observations of dyadic interactions in naturalistic settings

(Pederson, Gleason, Moran, & Bento, 1998; True, Pisani, & Oumar, 2001). Alternative attachment measures such as the Attachment Q-Sort have been widely used since the 1980s in homes rather than in the strange situation of the laboratory (Waters & Deane, 1985), but they do not receive mention by Vicedo.

Another issue of validity raised by Vicedo, and the particular focus of 'Putting attachment in its place', is the cross-cultural applicability of attachment theory and methods. The article continues the critique outlined in *The Nature and Nurture of Love*, that 'Whether in a poverty-stricken family in an African village, in a middle-class suburban American home, or in the very strange situation of an infant left alone with a stranger in a psychological laboratory, Ainsworth discerned the same "patterns of attachment behaviour".' (2013, p. 207). However, Vicedo seems unaware that the phrase 'patterns of attachment' changed meaning between the Uganda ethnography and the Baltimore study. In *Infancy in Uganda* (1967, p. 332), Ainsworth writes of 'differential crying' and 'lifting arms in greeting' as examples of patterns of 'attachment behaviour'. No claim was made that all children around the world show these behaviours when distressed. Indeed, Ainsworth's interest was in the fact that not even all children in the same family show these behaviours towards their caregiver, and that changes in family environment altered the likelihood of these behaviours being displayed. There is an important distinction between discrete behaviours and the organization of behaviours (Sroufe & Waters, 1977). The phrase 'patterns of attachment' was later repurposed by Ainsworth to refer to her classifications for the Strange Situation, but none of these are based necessarily on discrete behaviours. An infant can be classified as secure, for example, without ever approaching the caregiver or getting in contact; an infant can be classified as resistant without a display of anger. Indeed, these classifications were labeled A, B, and C by Ainsworth to avoid premature normative connotations with 'secure' or 'insecure' attachments. And later work by various researchers including Hinde, Main and Belsky emphasized the adaptive role of 'insecure' attachments in less than optimal rearing niches.

We know of no passage where Ainsworth stated an expectation that all infants would fit the three classifications found in her Baltimore study, and in a letter to Bowlby of the 10 March 1984 (Bowlby Archive PP/BOW/B.3/8) she stated explicitly that she was 'uneasy' at the very thought, and that further cross-cultural research would be needed before she would even take the proposal seriously. She was enthusiastic about cross-cultural research, for instance praising the work of her student Bob Marvin and colleagues for their study with the polymatric Hausa of Nigeria. In an interview, Ainsworth stated 'I think that environmental influences play no significant role in the infant's basic need for an attachment figure who can be trusted. But culture-related differences in ecologies and expectations will certainly affect how some specific aspects of that organization are expressed' (Ainsworth & Marvin, 1995, p. 8). Vicedo 'puts attachment in its place' in claiming that attachment researchers have failed to engage with cross-cultural research, but this claim is only possible because her analysis stops before the 1990s. She is right that there is need for further cross-cultural research, and attachment researchers have acknowledged this (e.g. Mesman et al., 2016). Yet decades of cross-cultural research have demonstrated the applicability of the Ainsworth classifications, though not their exhaustiveness. In 'Putting attachment in its place', Vicedo warmly cites claims that the Strange Situation 'cannot be used to study children in non-Western cultures' (2017, p. 690) but she ignores the large number of studies, reviewed in the *Handbook of Attachment*, conducted with the Strange Situation in a variety of non-WEIRD countries and cultures – including societies characterized by high levels of alloparenting. Cross-cultural attachment research does suggest that there are some general aspects to attachment, but this does not preclude very significant culture specific responses (Mesman et al., 2016). The relative cross-cultural validity of a research instrument and the cultural specificity of the things it seeks to measure does not represent a contradiction in terms, as Vicedo implies.

Disclosure statement

No potential conflict of interest was reported by the authors.

Funding

This work was supported by the Wellcome Trust [WT103343MA].

References

Ainsworth, M. (1967). *Infancy in uganda*. Baltimore: The Johns Hopkins Press.

Ainsworth, M. D. S., & Marvin, R. S. (1995). On the shaping of attachment theory and research: An interview with Mary D.S. Ainsworth (Fall 1994). *Monographs of the Society for Research in Child Development*, *60*(2–3), 3–21.

Bowlby, J. (1953). *Child Care and the Growth of Love*. Harmondsworth: Pelican.

Bowlby, J. (1969). *Attachment and Loss: Volume 1. Attachment*. New York: Basic Books.

Bowlby, J. (1991). Ethological light on psychoanalytic problems. In P. Bateson (Ed.), *The development and integration of behaviour* (pp. 301–314). Cambridge: Cambridge University Press.

Collins, H. (2004). *Gravity's shadow: The search for gravitational waves*. NY: Zone.

Cyr, C., Euser, E. M., Bakermans-Kranenburg, M. J., & van Ijzendoorn, M. H. (2010). Attachment security and disorganization in maltreating and high-risk families. *Development and Psychopathology*, *22*(1), 87–108.

Dozier, M., Kaufman, J., Kobak, R., O'Connor, T., Sagi-Schwartz, A., Scott, S., ... Zeanah, C.H. (2014). Consensus statement on group care for children and adolescents. *American Journal of Orthopsychiatry*, *84*, 219–225.

Goossens, F. A., & Ijzendoorn, M. H. (1990). Quality of infants' attachments to professional caregivers: Relation to infant-parent attachment and day-care characteristics. *Child Development*, *61*(3), 832–837.

Hrdy, S. B. (2009). Allomothers across Species, across Cultures, and through Time. In G. Bentley & R. Mace (Eds.), *Substitute parents: Biological and social perspectives on alloparenting in human societies*. Oxford: Berghan Books.

Lionetti, F., Pastore, M., & Barone, L. (2015). Attachment in institutionalized children: A review and meta-analysis. *Child Abuse & Neglect*, *42*, 135–145.

Mead, M. A. (1962). Cultural anthropologist's approach to maternal deprivation. *W.H. O. Public Health Papers*, No. 14, 45-62.

Mesman, J., van IJzendoorn, M. H., & Sagi-Schwartz, A. (2016). Cross-cultural patterns of attachment. In J. Cassidy & P. R. Shaver (Eds.), *The handbook of attachment: Theory, research, and clinical applications* (pp. 852–877). New York: The Guilford Press.

Mesman, J., van IJzendoorn, M., Behrens, K., Carbonell, O. A., Cárcamo, R., Cohen-Paraira, I., … Kondo-Ikemura, K. (2016b). Is the ideal mother a sensitive mother? *International Journal of Behavioral Development*, *40*(5), 385–397.

Midgley, N. (2014). The nature and nurture of love: From imprinting to attachment in cold War America. *Psychoanalysis & History*, *16*(2), 266–268.

Mooya, H., Sichimba, F., & Bakermans-Kranenburg, M. (2016). Infant–Mother and infant–Sibling attachment in Zambia. *Attachment & Human Development*, *18*(6), 618–635.

NICHD Early Child Care Research Network. (1997). The effects of infant child care on infant-mother attachment security. *Child Development*, *68*(5), 860–879.

Pederson, D. R., Gleason, K., Moran, G., & Bento, S. (1998). Maternal attachment representations, maternal sensitivity, and the infant–Mother attachment relationship. *Developmental Psychology*, *34*(1998), 925–933.

Plant, R. J. (2015). The nature and nurture of love: From imprinting to attachment in cold War America by Marga Vicedo. *Journal of Social History*, *49*(2), 456–459.

Pluess, M., & Belsky, J. (2009). Differential susceptibility to rearing experience: The case of childcare. *Journal of Child Psychology and Psychiatry*, *50*(4), 396–404.

Schickore, J., & Steinle, F. (Eds.). (2006). *Revisiting discovery and justification*. NY: Springer.

Sroufe, L. A., Egeland, B., Carlson, E. A., & Collins, W. A. (2005). The development of the person: The minnesota study of risk and adaptation from birth to adulthood. New York, NY: Guilford Press.

Sroufe, L. A., & Waters, E. (1977). Attachment as an organizational construct. *Child Development, 48*, 1184–1199.

True, M., Pisani, L., & Oumar, F. (2001). Infant–Mother attachment among the Dogon of Mali. *Child Development, 72*(5), 1451–1466.

Verhage, M. L., Schuengel, C., Madigan, S., Fearon, R. P., Oosterman, M., Cassibba, R., … van Ijzendoorn, M. H. (2016). Narrowing the transmission gap: A synthesis of three decades of research on intergenerational transmission of attachment. *Psychological Bulletin, 142*(4), 337–366.

Vicedo, M. (2013). *The nature and nurture of love: From imprinting to attachment in Cold War America.* Chicago: University of Chicago Press.

Vicedo, M. (2017). Putting attachment in its place: disciplinary and cultural contexts. *European Journal Of Developmental Psychology, 6*(14), 684-699.

Waters, E., & Deane, K. E. (1985). Defining and assessing individual differences in attachment relationships. *Monographs of the Society for Research in Child Development, 50*(1/2), 41–65.

On the history, present, and future of attachment theory: Reply to Robbie Duschinsky, Marinus van IJzendoorn, Sarah Foster, Sophie Reijman & Francesca Lionetti, 'Attachment histories and futures.'

Marga Vicedo

Discussing two of my publications on attachment theory, Duschinsky, Van IJzendoorn, Foster, Reijman, and Lionetti (2018) raise three points 'for sustaining a dialogue.' I welcome any dialogue on the important issues we need to study regarding children's development. I will address the three areas they cover: continuity in attachment theory over generations, the caregiving system, and the strange situation procedure. However, I focus on their main claim that I incorrectly 'assume uncomplicated continuity from attachment research from the mid-1950s to the present.'

The central question, then, is whether attachment theorists have discarded or even significantly modified the parts of the theory that I have criticized: John Bowlby's claims about the biological support for his ethological theory of attachment behavior and Bowlby's focus on mothers as primary caregivers. As I show below, this has not been the case.

Continuities or discontinuities across generations of researchers

First, Duschinsky et. al. claim that I miss the distinction between the context of discovery and the context of justification in science. As a result, they argue, I incorrectly treat evidence of the messy origin of ideas about attachment as 'evidence of their lack of scientific validity.' That is not correct. I did not critique Bowlby's views because of their messy origins. I criticized the lack of empirical evidence for them.

Interestingly, Duschinsky and his colleagues agree: 'We fully acknowledge that most of Bowlby's ideas were not well grounded in adequate supporting evidence, were influenced by contemporary ideologies, and that caution is needed in using those that have not seen adequate testing' (Duschinsky et al., 2018). I welcome their willingness to move beyond uncritical reverence for the founders of attachment theory, Bowlby and Mary Ainsworth, and toward empirical testing of core assumptions of attachment theory.

Unfortunately, however, many of their colleagues do not share that willingness. This is apparent by reading through several editions of the *Handbook of Attachment*. For example, in her paper about the history of attachment theory and research, June Cassidy still states in the recent last edition: 'Bowlby and Ainsworth's original ideas have held up well.' Thus, she concludes: '... nothing that has emerged from the thousands of studies produced over the past 40 years has led to a serious challenge to the core theory' (Cassidy, 2018, p. 17).

So prominent researchers such as Cassidy claim there is continuity. Their insistence that Bowlby's and Ainsworth's ideas are still valid is what makes my criticisms of their views relevant to current attachment research.

Second, Duschinsky et. al. contest my view that Bowlby's attachment theory focuses on children's attachment to their mother. They claim that in the mid 1960s, Bowlby gave up the idea that mother love is instinctual and that it is necessary for the mother to be a 'child's sole attachment figure.' I don't think there is evidence to support this position.

Bowlby maintained that there is always one primordial attachment figure. As he put it: 'Because the bias of a child to attach himself especially to one figure seems to be well established and also to have far-reaching implications for psychopathology, I believe it merits a special term. In the earlier paper I referred to it as "monotropy"' (Bowlby, 1969, 1982, p. 309). Bowlby also stated throughout his writings that this figure is usually the mother. That, combined with the fact that the empirical work on which he relied focused on mothers, made any other 'figure' just a figure of speech, literally.

Take, for example, the paper Duschinsky et. al. cite as evidence for Bowlby's acceptance of distributive care (Bowlby, 1991). The quotation they use comes from a paragraph in which Bowlby is talking about attachment behavior as a characteristic of many species. When he starts discussing humans in the next full paragraph, he talks about the internal working models of the child and his or her mother (p. 307). In the next section, he talks about three patterns of attachment, one leading to a child 'developing healthily' and the two others being 'predictive of disturbed development.' Here he refers to parents, parent-type figures, and mothers. The secure pattern is found, he says, 'to be promoted by a parent, in the early years especially by the mother, being readily available, sensitive to her child's signals and lovingly responsive when protection and/or comfort and/or assistance is sought.' The anxious resistant attachment results, he says, when the child is uncertain whether a 'parent' will be responsive. The third pattern, anxious avoidant attachment, he notes, 'is the result of their mothers constantly rebuffing them when approached for comfort or protection' (Bowlby, 1991, p. 308).Thus, in his last paper, as in his other publications, Bowlby referred to the mother-figure, and to the parents. But, mostly, he referred to the mothers. Moreover, the empirical studies he cited, even in this last paper, focus on children's attachment to their mothers.

Furthermore, Bowlby argued that maternal caregiving behavior is instinctual (Bowlby 1958; Bowlby, 1969, 1982). This was a central claim in his ethological theory of attachment. For Bowlby, the attachment system is composed of two sub-systems: the caregiving system and the child's attachment system (Bowlby, 1969, 1982, p. 182). According to him, the attachment system is an adaptation designed by natural selection in the environment of evolutionary adaptedness (EEA). Elsewhere I have argued that Bowlby's evolutionary interpretation of the attachment system committed him to view maternal care as basically instinctual (Vicedo, 2017a).

Third, Duschinsky et. al. accuse me of 'partiality' because I describe Margaret Mead's criticism that Bowlby saw maternal care as necessary for a child's healthy emotional development, but did not provide 'Bowlby's direct reply to it.' I claimed that Bowlby did not answer her criticisms, noting that he 'mentioned Mead only once in a footnote, just to state briefly she had misunderstood him (Bowlby, 1969, 1982, p. 303). However, he offered no explanation or rebuttal of her arguments' (Vicedo, 2017b, p. 687). This is an accurate description of what Bowlby did.

Fourth, Duschinsky et. al. also challenge my view that most attachment researchers have continued to focus mainly on mothers. However, numerous anthropologists and psychologists have pointed this out over a number of years (for references see Keller & Chaudhary, 2017).

Finally, it is perhaps worth noting that their claim that both 'historians and psychologists' have criticized my assumption of continuity is an exaggeration. As evidence, they refer to only two reviews of my book *The Nature and Nurture of Love*, by Midgley (2014) and Plant (2015). Those reviewers are not critical of my historical work. Midgley believes that my 'critique of attachment as a purely behavioural/biological theory is somewhat outdated' (Midgley, 2014, p. 268) This would be true if attachment theorists had rejected that part of the theory in recent decades. But I have not seen evidence they have done so. Plant characterizes my book as 'a rigorous critique of the theory's central claims and founding works,' and 'a major contribution to the history of the psychological sciences' (Plant 2015, p. 457). But she also notes that, despite its shaky foundation," attachment theory could contain valid elements." Specifically, she says: 'One can jettison the idea of mother love as instinctual, as well as the fixation on the mother as the crucial attachment figure, without discarding all of the theory's insights about stages of attachment or the importance of humans' earliest relationships in establishing patterns that shape subsequent interpersonal relationships' (Plant 2015, p. 459). I agree with her point. Yet, the idea of mother love as instinctual is central to Bowlby's ethological theory of attachment. And the fixation on the mother continues in much of attachment research.

The caregiving system

In this section, Duschinsky et al. present two main criticisms.

One is that I do not understand that the caregiving system behavioral system is a 'different construct (conceptually and evolutionarily) from the child attachment system.' I have never claimed otherwise. The two systems are different, first of all empirically, and then also 'conceptually and evolutionarily.'

Two, they say that I ignore recent attachment research in different contexts. According to them, that work shows how the caregiving system 'is dependent on social and cultural processes, leading to situation-specificity.' They recommend that I pay attention to the work of Mesman and colleagues. In fact, in collaboration with some psychologists and anthropologists, I have done so. Our conclusion, simply stated, is that those studies do not take culture seriously (Keller et al., 2018). In our view, much of that research sees culture as an added layer that simply shapes pre-programmed patterns that are regarded as uniform and universal. In addition, in their paper, Duschinsky et al. only acknowledge that culture influences the caregiving system. But we argue that culture interacts with the development of the child's attachment system, as well.

For us, culture is an intrinsic component of a child's attachments to others and of a caregiver's behavior. In interaction with socio-economic, biological, and ecological factors, culture helps conform a wide variety of behaviors and emotions that are not adequately recognized in current attachment theory (Morelli et al., 2017; Keller & Bard, 2017).

The strange situation procedure

Given that I cannot adequately discuss all the points raised about this topic, I cover only three issues briefly.

First, Duschinsky et. al. write: 'Vicedo argues that reliance on the Strange Situation has meant that researchers "led developmental psychologists to a distorted vision of children because it ignored the role of context in child development." (2017: 689).' However, the full sentence of my article says: 'In sum, critical voices pointed out that the reliance on laboratory experiments led developmental psychologists to a distorted vision of children because it ignored the role of context in child development' (Vicedo 1017b, pp. 689–90). In other words, my assertion is a historical claim about how some psychologists, specifically Urie Bronfenbrenner and William Kessen, saw the general methodological reliance on experiments in psychology as detrimental to the goal of reaching a full understanding of children's development. I provide the specific references to these authors, so readers can see that my historical claim is accurate.

Second, I am accused of being unaware that the phrase 'patterns of attachment' changed meaning between the Uganda ethnography and the Baltimore study. Duschinsky et al. note that 'discrete behaviours and the organization of behaviours' are two different things. Indeed, I have not said otherwise in any of my writings. More to the point, my criticism of Ainsworth's work is not based on a misunderstanding of her concepts.

Instead, my criticism is the following: The ethnographic work Ainsworth carried out in Uganda (Ainsworth, 1967) was not robust enough to support her conclusions (see Vicedo, 2013). In addition, the conclusions that Ainsworth and her collaborators drew from the Baltimore study and the Strange Situation procedure (Ainsworth, Blehar, Waters, & Wall, 1978) have been thoroughly criticized for their methodological shortcomings and unsupported assumptions (e.g., Lamb, Thompson, Gardner, Charnov, & Estes, 1984). Moreover, having now reviewed in the archives the original data collected in the Baltimore study, I do not believe any scholar would consider the notes taken by the diverse observers during home visits reliable scientific data. Although I do not yet have permission from the archives to cite the data, concerned scholars can review the original material and form their own opinion. Ideally, a team of researchers would examine those records carefully and present a critical analysis of their adequacy.

Since the organizational constructs used in attachment research to categorize a child's attachment (secure, anxious resistant, anxious avoidant, ambivalent) were developed using those original, flawed data, I do not think the SSP is a scientifically valid instrument for examining a child's attachments. In itself, when correctly administered and interpreted, the SSP could be used in many contexts to illuminate children's behavior. In my view, however, the categories and conclusions that Ainsworth et al. 1978 reached with the SSP are not scientifically defensible. They relied on unsound data, faulty methodology, and unproven assumptions about children's behavior as reliable markers of their own and their caretakers' feelings and conduct.

In sum, I do not assume that a research instrument cannot be cross-culturally reliable and valid. For me, the SSP is not a scientifically sound procedure to measure the quality of children's attachments or to reach conclusions about their caregivers – in any culture.

Conclusion

Children form attachments. Many of those attachments influence different aspects of their development, in various and complex ways.

Bowlby and Ainsworth developed a theory to account for such phenomena: the ethological theory of attachment. Its central claim was that the attachment system is an adaptation. As Ainsworth put it: 'The great strength of attachment theory in guiding research is that it focuses on a basic system of behavior–the attachment system–that is biologically rooted and thus species-characteristic' (Ainsworth, 1991, p. 33). Mesman et. al. (2016, p. 804) have asserted: 'The cross-cultural studies included here support Bowlby's (1969/1982) idea that attachment is indeed a universal phenomenon, and an evolutionary explanation seems to be warranted.' (See Vicedo, 2017a for a discussion of how universality does not warrant an evolutionary explanation). And Cassidy (2018, p. 4) still maintains: 'The most fundamental aspect of attachment theory is its focus on the biological bases of attachment behavior (Bowlby, 1958, 1969/1982).'

I have argued that Bowlby's views about the biology of attachment have thus far not been substantiated. Other attachment researchers have modified them by introducing the notion of conditional strategies and the belief that alloparenting was probably widespread in early human evolution. Yet, these ideas are still only theoretical proposals. In fact, Main introduced some of them in what she herself characterized as a 'speculative' essay (Main, 1990, p. 48). I have also argued that current and more sophisticated suggestions to shore up the alleged biological basis of attachment remain in the realm of speculation (Vicedo, 2017a). Science needs speculations. It moves forward by proposals that need to be tested. However, it is important not to present speculative ideas as support for the validity of a theory. As of today, the ethological theory of attachment cannot claim that biological science proves or even provides adequate evidence for its main tenets.

Attachment theory has evolved over time, as any scientific theory does and should do. Thus, Duschinsky et al. put their finger on a crucial question: What is the relationship between current attachment theory and Bowlby's and Ainsworth's ideas?

Thompson (2017) provides an overview of the many criticisms that attachment theory received over the last several decades. He reviews the changes in attachment research in order to offer a 'portrayal of twenty-first century attachment theory' (303). In addition, he surveys the various ways in which attachment researchers now try to incorporate the cultural context in which relationships develop.

However, nowhere in his paper does he tell us how this research has led to modifications of the core theory. We are thus left with an overview of different areas of research, but no coherent picture of what 'twenty-first century attachment theory' encompasses.

Duschinsky et al. accuse me of conflating Bowlby's ideas with more recent and current attachment theory and research. At this point, I have two simple questions for them: Which flaws in Bowlby's and Ainsworth's empirical, conceptual, and theoretical work have attachment scholars acknowledged and decided to reject or to modify? And, what is attachment theory today?

Disclosure statement

No potential conflict of interest was reported by the author.

References

Ainsworth, M. D. S. (1967). *Infancy in Uganda: Infant care and the growth of love*. Baltimore, MD: Johns Hopkins University Press.

Ainsworth, M. D. S. (1991). Attachments and other affectional bonds across the life cycle. In C. Murray Parkes, J. Stevenson-Hinde, & P. Harris (Eds.), *Attachment across the life cycle* (pp. 33–51). London: Routledge.

Ainsworth, M. D. S., Blehar, M. C., Waters, E., & Wall, S. (1978). *Patterns of attachment: A psychological study of the strange situation*. Hillsdale, NJ: Erlbaum.

Bowlby, J. (1958). The nature of the child's tie to his mother. *International Journal of Psychoanalysis*, *39*, 350–373.

Bowlby, J. (1969, 1982). *Attachment*. New York: Basic Books.

Bowlby, J. (1991). Ethological light on psychoanalytic problems. In P. Bateson (Ed.), *The development and integration of behaviour* (pp. 301–313). Cambridge: Cambridge University Press.

Cassidy, J. (2018). The nature of the child's ties. In J. Cassidy & P. R. Shaver (Eds.), *Handbook of attachment: Theory, research and clinical applications* (3rd ed., pp. 3–24). New York: Guilford.

Duschinsky, R., van IJzendoorn, M., Foster, S., Reijman, S., & Lionetti, F. (2018). *Attachment histories and futures*. European Journal of Developmental Psychology.

Keller, H., & Chaudhary, N. (2017). Is the mother essential for attachment? Models of care in different cultures. In H. Keller & K. A. Bard (Eds.), *The cultural nature of attachment* (pp. 109–137). Cambridge, MA: MIT Press.

Keller, H., Bard, K., Morelli, G., Chaudhary, N., Vicedo, M., Rosabal-Coto, M., ... Gottlieb, A. (2018). The myth of universal sensitive responsiveness: Comment on Mesman et al. (2017). Child Development. Advance online publication. doi:10.1111/cdev.13031.

Keller, H., & Bard, K. A. (Eds.). (2017). *The cultural nature of attachment*. Cambridge, MA: MIT Press.

Lamb, M. E., Thompson, R. A., Gardner, W. P., Charnov, E. L., & Estes, D. (1984). Security of infantile attachment as assessed in the "strange situation": Its study and biological interpretation. *The Behavioral and Brain Sciences*, *7*, 127–147.

Main, M. (1990). Cross-cultural studies of attachment organization: Recent studies, changing methodologies, and the concept of conditional strategies. *Human Development*, *33*, 48–61.

Mesman, J., van Ijzendoorn, M., & Sagi-Schwartz, A. (2016). Cross-cultural patterns of attachment. In J. Cassidy & P. R. Shaver (Eds.), *The handbook of attachment: Theory, research, and clinical applications* (pp. 852–877). New York: The Guilford Press.

Midgley, N. (2014). Review of the war inside and of the nature and nurture of love: From imprinting to attachment in Cold War America. *Psychoanalysis & History*, *16*(2), 266–268.

Morelli, G., Chaudhary, N., Gottlieb, A., Keller, H., Murray, M., Quinn, N., ... Vicedo, M. (2017). Taking culture seriously: A pluralistic approach to attachment. In H. Keller & K. A. Bard (Eds.), *The cultural nature of attachment* (pp. 139–169). Cambridge, MA: MIT Press.

Plant, R. J. (2015). Review of the nature and nurture of love by Marga Vicedo. *Journal of Social History*, *49*(2), 456–459.

Thompson, R. A. (2017). Twenty-First century attachment theory: Challenges and opportunities. In H. Keller & K. A. Bard (Eds.), *The cultural nature of attachment* (pp. 301–319). Cambridge, MA: MIT Press.

Vicedo, M. (2013). *The nature and nurture of love. From imprinting to attachment in Cold War America*. Chicago, IL: The University of Chicago Press.

Vicedo, M. (2017a). The strange situation of the ethological theory of attachment in historical perspective. In H. Keller & K. A. Bard (Eds.), *The cultural nature of attachment* (pp. 13–51). Cambridge, MA: MIT Press.

Vicedo, M. (2017b). Putting attachment in its place: Disciplinary and cultural contexts. *European Journal of Developmental Psychology*, *14*(6), 684–699.

Cultural and historical diversity in early relationship formation

Heidi Keller

ABSTRACT

Attachment theory has been challenged as representing exclusively Western middle class child care philosophy. In particular, the conception of a single, primary adult caregiver does not correspond with the reality of many early child care patterns worldwide. Different models of care that have been identified and described by cultural anthropologists, cultural and cross-cultural psychologists over the last decades are presented. It is apparent that in many cultural communities children and grandparents are significant caretakers and attachment figures. Caregiving is adapted to the sociocultural environments in which children are born and raised to become competent adults. Sociocultural environments also change over historical time, especially with respect to the amount of formal schooling and, as a corollary, maternal age at first birth, the number of children in the household, and household composition. In the second part of the paper, sociodemographic changes in different cultural environments are documented. Concomitant changes in socialization goals and socialization strategies involving babies are presented; these involve comparing different generations (mothers and grandmothers), and different cohorts over historical time. In the discussion the interplay between change and continuity as related constructs for understanding human development and well-being is considered, along with how universality and cultural/historical specificity co-exist in early relationship formation and thus attachment.

Introduction

The human lifespan can be understood as patterned by developmental tasks which evolved during the history of humankind in order to solve adaptive problems faced by our ancestors. Thus, developmental tasks are part of the human condition that defines the universal nature of humankind. The development of attachment relationships is one of the earliest developmental tasks during human ontogeny. Human infants are born prematurely (condition of altriciality) due to hominid brain development (the obstetrical dilemma). They are therefore dependent on a caring environment that helps them to develop competence in the particular environment into which they are born. Attachment relationships can be regarded as mediating the development of competence and agency. They represent avenues to learning and information processing.

In order to execute developmental tasks, humans are equipped with a universal repertoire of behavioral dispositions that allow for contextually sensitive solutions. To facilitate the development of attachment relationships, infants are equipped with morphological characteristics as well as behavioral dispositions that elicit care. A parenting co-design to care, stimulate and console infants is equally central to the evolved behavioral repertoire, a pattern already apparent in small children interacting with babies (Keller, 2007; Keller & Kärtner, 2013).

Although John Bowlby (1969) had assumed evolutionary origins for the formation of attachment, however, he did not realize that a crucial assumption of evolutionary theorizing relates to differential effects of the environment in shaping phenotypes. Based on the Western middle-class conception of family, Bowlby (1969), later joined by the Canadian psychologists Mary Ainsworth (1967), promoted the view of monotropy as a universal mechanism. Monotropy assumes that attachment is an intimate and vital bond of a child with one specific, particular attachment figure, usually the mother (Bowlby, 1988). In this view, the mother-infant relationship is unique and therefore qualitatively different from all other relationships the child may form; as such it has profound consequences for children's development as a whole. The relationship is considered to represent a specific emotional connection that the individual develops during the first year of life on the basis of the interactional experiences with that particular caregiver. Although current attachment researchers deny the assumption of monotropy, they nevertheless maintain the assumption of one primary caregiver (who who might be supported by a few others), who is an adult and still primarily the mother (Keller & Chaudhary, 2016). As argued below this particular scenario of attachment development is an exception rather than the rule on a worldwide scale.

The second misconception of the Bowlby-Ainsworth view of the evolutionary basis of attachment formation is that parenting quality is assumed to take the same form of (maternal) sensitivity universally; this view is complemented more recently with the concept of mind-mindedness (Meins et al., 2002). This view assumes a secure attachment relationship, the gold standard for the start of a healthy, happy and competent developmental trajectory, can only emerge when the child experiences unconditional, dyadic, and exclusive attention. Thus even minimal infant signals need to be answered responsively and sensitively (an assumption of contingency) so that the child can develop a sense of predictability and thus agency (Ainsworth, Blehar, Waters, & Wall, 1978). Besides signs of distress, especially signals in the face-to-face context are assumed to be critical. The verbalization and interpretation of the infant's inner state, needs, wishes and intentions, cognitions and emotions by the primary attachment figure are assumed to support the development of an early sense of agency and self-worth. Correspondingly, from the adult perspective, the belief is that the mother finds herself primarily bonded towards a single child at a time (Minde, Corter, Goldberg, & Jeffers, 1990).

In contrast to these assumptions, however, when care of children is regarded across time and space, it becomes evident that monotropy and the unconditional exclusive attention of one primary adult caregiver is predicated upon several conditions. In order for the mother to devote exclusive attention towards a single child, she must be ensured of her own safety and survival, the child's survival, a stable environment free of imminent dangers, food security, moderate temperature, and many other conditions that a modern home offers. Such conditions permit exclusive attention by leaving the adult free from other life-saving or life-sustaining tasks. As a corollary, the high level of formal education of middle-class mothers allows and promotes a particular, i.e., distal style of interactional exchange with abundant face-to-face contact and object stimulation embedded in a voluminous conversational stream.

It is the premise of evolutionary theorizing that behavior, including care arrangements for children, are adapted to the environmental context in which families live. Understood within that framework, the particular pocket of the world's population that lives in affluence and has high degrees of formal education as the necessary environment for the formation of attachment in the Bowlby-Ainsworth tradition is rather small. Yet that small segment is grossly overrepresented in research and theorizing regarding early relationship formation. Conversely, cultural anthropologists and psychologists have accumulated substantial evidence that the 'neglected 95%' (Arnett, 2008) live in significantly different circumstances with diverse care arrangements.

Alternative models of care

A far more frequent model of care is alloparenting. This pattern is widely distributed across different modes of subsistence and living arrangements, such as farmers, hunter-gatherers, fishermen, pastorals, but also non-Western urban families. In fact, the involvement in child care of others – especially grandmothers, older siblings, fathers but also unrelated kin – on a routine basis can be regarded as a human universal going back to the appearance of homo erectus (Burkart & van Schaik, 2010). Moreover, the coordination of different tasks simultaneously as a daily challenge of many women in the world necessitates caregiving mainly as co-occurring activity (Saraswathi & Pai, 1997). Carrying a baby on the hips or the back is a mode of caretaking that allows free movement and usage of both hands at the same time. And carrying involves channels of communication other than face-to-face exchange, so that interactional regulations (e.g., behavioral contingencies) are expressed primarily proximally through body contact and touching (e.g., Chapin, 2013). However, given that mothers cannot carry infants all the time because of the need to balance energetic investment and domestic activities, the motivation for alloparental carrying of infants is crucial, since leaving children alone would pose too much risk, e.g., from predators (Keller & Chaudhary, 2016).

Multiple caregiving can consist of a multiplicity of arrangements of caretakers and responsibilities. The mother may play a special role among other caregivers, or be equal to others, or may not be a special caretaker at all. Moreover, these arrangements can vary over time. For example, when they are four months of age Aka and Efe hunter-gatherer infants are transferred to different people seven to eight times per hour, and are held by seven to 14 different individuals during 8-h observation periods. Overall Aka children exhibit attachment behaviors to about six of the 20 people with whom they are in daily contact during the first year (Meehan & Hawks, 2013). As another example, anthropologist Gabriel Scheidecker has described the socialization experiences of village children in the South of Madagascar where mothers play a special role in infants' life during the first two years and completely disappear thereafter. Moreover, children from that age on are not exposed to adults but develop in the context of peer groups (Scheidecker, 2014).

Another abrupt change of the caregiving environment has been described by Cora DuBois (1944) for the Alorese community. There the nurturing relationship during the first year of life suddenly declines to complete inattention by the mother and even to the point of potential food deprivation, a condition that attachment theory would consider as a major precursor of psychopathology (Cassidy, 2008). But the opposite pattern may also occur. Hewlett (1991) describes for the Aka a dramatic decline in allomothering over the first year of age. By eight months of age, Aka infants receive substantially less care from others and relatively more care from the mother.

In yet another cultural variation, the primary attachment figure may not be the biological mother at all. Among the Nigerian Hausa, mothers live together and share childcare responsibilities. Hausa infants seem to become attached with the person who interacted most with him or her, which in eight of 14 observed cases was not the biological mother (Marvin, Van Devender, Iwanaga, LeVine, & LeVine, 1977).

In many cultural environments, from the moment of birth on, infants are passed on to other caretakers. Among the Efe, the mother may not be the first to nurse an infant, while others participate in nursing during early infancy (Tronick, Morelli, & Winn, 1987). And Aka mothers are not the first to touch and hold an infant. An older female-in-law cleans the infant and takes it to the hut until the mother arrives, since Aka women give birth outside their camps (Hewlett, 1991). Thus, multiple attachment relationships may be developed simultaneously that are similar in importance and significance (Morelli, 2015).

Multiple caregiving may be the dominant mode in particular contexts, as in the case of Aka hunter-gatherers when they are in a camp. At other times, for example during foraging activities like net hunting, the mother is the dominant caretaker (Hewlett, 1991).

In yet another variation, siblings, or polymatric caregiving, may characterize over 90% of the infant care that is not provided by the mother. Siblings mostly care for infants when they are older than 2 months of age. In Nigerian families, small children interact with other children 48% of the time as compared with 10–15% of interaction with the mother, leading to strong attachment relationships among siblings (Fatimilehini & Hassan, 2015).

Besides sibling care, grandparenting is probably the most common mode of alloparenting. Grandmaternal involvement is usually higher than grandpaternal involvement because the maternal grandmother can be sure that she is investing in her genetic offspring, whereas grandfathers can never be sure in whom they invest due to paternity insecurity (Voland, Chasiotis, & Schiefenhövel, 2004). Grandmothering is best considered an adaptation through which aging females achieve better fitness returns than continuing to produce and rear their own offspring (Hawkes, O'Connell, Blurton Jones, Alvarez, & Charnov, 2008). The extended lifespan beyond the reproductive years is assumed to allow older women to effectively help in rearing grandchildren (Lancy, 2008).

Although these evolutionary considerations apply to all grandmothers irrespective of cultural background, the role and engagement of grandmothers vary considerably across cultures. For example, Chinese culture values the involvement of grandparents in caregiving (Mjelde-Mossey, 2007), especially with respect to child-feeding practices (Xie & Xia, 2011). Direct involvement is common in rural farming families, for example in Turkey, where grandmothers raise children alongside mothers. Grandmothers in Western middle-class families, in contrast, are more likely to understand their role as being fun partners for their grandchildren and to spend leisurely time with them. They do not consider themselves as educational authorities (Lamm & Teiser, 2013).

Different caregivers may embody different roles for children's development. The mother may be responsible for nursing the baby, whereas siblings play and stimulate with their charges, and the kind of care provided can and does differ from person to person.

Historical changes

Since they are created and co-created individually as well as collectively, cultures are dynamic systems. Therefore, they also change over historical time. Historical epochs within and across sociocultural milieus thus represent cultural environments with distinct values, ideas, and practices. Caregiving patterns and arrangements also change over historical time. Marga Vicedo (2013) has demonstrated convincingly how attachment theory itself is bound to historical time and circumstances.

Changes in the cultures of caregiving are driven by changes in sociodemographic parameters, especially an increase in formal education and related changes in age at first birth, number of children, and household composition. Changes in these characteristics can be observed in surveys worldwide. In a comparative study we have assessed sociodemographic variables of mothers and their mothers in cultural communities that adhere to different childcare philosophies (Lamm, Keller, Yovsi, & Chaudhary, 2008; see Table 1).

Table 1 indicates that formal education increases from one generation to the next in contexts as diverse as rural and urban Cameroonian Nso, urban middle-class Indians, and urban middle-class Germans. The mean number of children decreases and household composition also changes accordingly. Nevertheless, the changes vary in magnitude and also in rapidity from context to context. In the non-Western families, rural as well as urban, the changes in household size are small, indicating that the family structure may remain similar over generations. Moreover, numbers may mean different things. Changing from illiteracy to seven years of basic formal education may imply different psychological and social changes than a seven-year increase in formal education in a highly formally educated environment.

Such sociodemographic parameters form particular milieus that can be associated with different caregiving philosophies (Keller, 2007; Keller & Kärtner, 2013). Individuals with higher education tend to be economically more affluent and thus independent from outer constraints than individuals with less formal education. They place greater emphasis on verbal expression and inner psychological states than behavior. Fewer children in the family allow exclusive attention to the individual child which is embodied in a distal mode of interaction with abundant cognitive stimulation. Relationships are negotiated emotionally. In contrast, less formally educated individuals tend to interact more physically with small children, with extensive body contact and motor stimulation. Verbal interactions are more restrictive and repetitive emphasizing social domains, conventional codes, and moral standards (e.g., Schröder, Keller, & Kleis, 2013).

In a study comparing maternal and grandmaternal ethnotheories about childrearing in different cultural environments, we interviewed mothers and grandmothers from the same families (see Table 1) with a picture-based qualitative interview. We documented changes between the generations in emphasis regarding content of caregiving as well as styles of narrating about caregiving in line with the sociodemographic profiles (Lamm et al., 2008).

The most pronounced differences were reported between urban Cameroonian Nso mothers and grandmothers, reflecting a dramatic change in living conditions from rural subsistence-based farming with high illiteracy rates in the grandmother generation to highly educated urban middle-class women

Table 1. Change of sociodemographic parameters from generation to generation.

	Mothers				Grand-mothers			
	Berlin	Delhi	Urban Nso	Rural Nso	Berlin	Delhi	Urban Nso	Rural Nso
Years of formal education	15.3	15.5	12.9	6.7	11.6	12.3	3.2	1.0
Mean number of children	1.4	1.6	2.6	3.4	2.5	2.9	5.8	5.9
Number of persons per household	3.5	6.1	6.7	7.5	2.1	6.4	7.3	6.3

of their daughters. Among the samples assessed in the study this group was the only one demonstrating substantial changes in explicitly formulated ideas about parenting, with mothers focusing far more on distal (face-to-face, object stimulation) strategies of parenting than grandmothers. However, there were no differences in the discourse style of urban Nso mothers and grandmothers. This may indicate that, compared to nonverbal means of communication, language traditionally may be not as important as a cultural medium for Nso education and that such changes may only occur beyond one generation (Keller, 2007).

There were no differences in the parenting ethnotheories of rural Nso mothers and grandmothers. Although all mothers had completed almost seven years of primary school education as compared with virtually no formal education in the grandmother generation, mothers – like the grandmothers – still lived the same lifestyle based on subsistence farming in the same household. Thus intergenerational continuity did not necessitate, and may also not permit, changing child rearing philosophies.

The mothers in both Berlin and Delhi differed from the grandmother generations more in the way they expressed their general ideas about parenting than in the content domains they explicitly mentioned. The discourse style of the mothers became more self-centered, referring more to mental states, whereas the grandmothers placed more emphasis on social topics and conventions. However, the similarities in the content domains of mothers and grandmothers of the two groups may be brought about by different dynamics. It is also apparent that the grandmothers in both settings had high degrees of formal education (more than 10 years) which is associated with a preference for distal parenting (Keller, 2007).

Moreover, specific features of the two contexts may drive the similarities in content. In the Delhi sample, 92% of the mother–grandmother pairs lived in the same household and practiced collective care of children. In order to maintain family harmony it would make sense that similar strategies are emphasized.

The Berlin grandmothers, in contrast, seem to have adapted their parenting strategies towards their daughters. Keller and Demuth (2005), who had also found similarities between Berlin grandmothers and mothers in a qualitative study, suggest that, in a society where kinship is no longer a necessary bond, grandmothers have adapted their views to their daughters in order to maintain regular contact and rewarding relationships with their children and thus grandchildren. A similar pattern had also been described for Euro-American mother–grandmother pairs (Cho, Sandel, Miller, & Wang, 2005). Euro-American grandmothers explicitly mentioned that they did not want to give child-rearing advice to their daughters or violate their autonomy as mothers. Such an interpretation is also supported by the self-understanding of grandmothers referred to earlier. That is, Western middle-class grandmothers do not regard themselves as educational partners of their grandchildren. Moreover, the fast-changing historical pace between generations in the Western world may contribute to such differences in strategies and philosophies. Each generation is literally living in a different world where their own ideas and practices regarding child care and education may not be appropriate for preparing the grandchild generation for adult competence.

In conclusion, these studies suggest a transcultural change process involving a cultural model oriented more towards psychological autonomy of the individual as a result of increasing formal education and urban life style. Mothers' ethnotheories focus more on independent functioning of the individual, whereas grandmothers' ethnotheories place greater emphasis on interpersonal relationships and harmonious functioning of the group. These differences are expressed differently in both behavioral content and narrating styles.

Another way of assessing historical changes involves the cross-sectional comparison of samples over historical time. As an example, Keller, Borke, Yovsi, Lohaus, and Jensen (2005) compared the interactional behavior with their three-months-old babies of Nso farmer and German middle-class mothers from cohorts four–six years apart. In line with the ethnotheory study described above, there was no change in Nso farmer mothers' interactional behavior across this short time span. German mothers, on the other hand, showed substantial changes, with a significant increase in object stimulation and a significant decrease in motor/body stimulation.

Moreover, we were fortunate to be able to study interactional behavior between German middle-class mothers and their first-born infants in two comparable cohorts about 20 years apart (Keller & Lamm, 2005). The mothers of our older sample (cohort 1) had their first child in 1977/1978. The mothers of our younger sample (cohort 2) had their first child in 2000. Substantial societal changes had occurred between these two epochs that are mirrored in sociodemographic statistics. Most important, formal education had increased significantly between the two time-spans. The number of university students in West Germany had increased from about 1.04 million in 1980 to 1.63 million in 2001. And the percentage of women studying at a university had increased from 36.7 in 1980 to 46.1 in 2000. Women's participation in the labor force had also increased from 36.4% (women with children under six years of age) in 1980 to 52.9% in 2001. There were several parallel patterns – The number of marriages had declined (6.3 per 1000 inhabitants in 1980 to 5.1 in 2000) and divorce rates had increased (from 1.8 per 1000 inhabitants in 1980 to 2.4 in 2000). The average age of marriage became delayed for women, from 23.4 in 1980 to 28.5 in 2000, and for men from 26.1 in 1980 to 31.3 in 2000. The average age of mothers when their first child is born had increased from 25.2 in 1980 to 28.9 in 1999. During this time children lived in only one in three households in Germany (All figures from the Statistisches Bundesamt, Wiesbaden, Germany. All figures represent the national level of the Western part of Germany so that it can be expected that numbers representing middle-class only would be even more dramatic).

Overall, these developments reflect an increasing complexity of urban lifestyles, the pluralization of roles and greater social differentiation, and reduced standardization of society. All these changes amount to the definition of individuality as a social demand on each member of a society (Heitmeyer & Olk, 1995; Sünker, 1995).

These changes can also be assumed to affect the nature of parent–child relationships, since parents want to prepare their children for competence in their future lives. Indeed, our data confirm that the two generations of mothers differ in their interactional patterns with their 3-month-old babies. The younger generation of mothers provide their infants with significantly more distal contingency experiences, i.e., prompt reactions to infant's facial cues and object play; at the same time expressions of warmth, both bodily closeness as well as smiling and baby talk, decreased. Fathers changed their interactional behaviors similarly over the same time period (Eickhorst, Lamm, Borke, & Keller, 2008).

Overall, these results indicate broad changes related to global individualism. Self-determination, self-containment and a psychologically inward turn characterize competence in the complexity of urban environments. These results are also consistent with findings of a study that compared Turkish urban upper middle-class grandmothers', mothers', and daughters' perceptions of their parents' child-rearing attitudes (Sever, 1989). The reported decreased emphasis on authoritarian control and increased emphasis on encouraging independence, open expression, and expression of affect were similarly associated with social changes in the Turkish society.[1] Also, a French three-generation study on family values (Sabatier & Lannegrand-Willem, 2005) revealed that mothers focus on modern values (individualism and autonomy) and grandmothers on traditional values (collectivism and obedience). With continuing intergenerational change, adolescents were more individualistic than their mothers. Similar observations have been made by the Norwegian anthropologist Marianne Gullestad who related '... present changes in theories of management and worklife ... (to) ... changes from a popular rhetorical emphasis on "obedience" to an emphasis on "being oneself" in the upbringing of children ...' (1996, p. 25). And an analysis

[1]It remains to be seen whether and how more recent socio-political changes in Turkey lead to yet another shift in parenting/family practices.

of autobiographies of Norwegian women revealed that family practices related to obedience are linked to the 'positional family' (where family roles and power structures are rigid), whereas family practices related to 'being oneself' are linked to the 'person-centered family' (where the members are recognized as individuals and roles are negotiated) (Bernstein, 1971; Gullestad, 1996).

Finally, Elder, Modell, and Parke (1993) underlined that across the twentieth century, each generation of American children has come of age in a different world of realities, realities that are expressed in the dynamics of family relationships. Each generation modifies the ideas about child rearing, proper care, and socialization goals that are pursued in their parents' generation. These changes pertain to all developmental domains and shape children's developmental trajectories. Similarly, Patricia Greenfield (2004) has convincingly demonstrated how changed lifestyles, especially the transition from subsistence to cash economy in a Mexican village in Chiapas, altered learning styles and consequently children's cognitive development. She also demonstrated that individual creativity emerged at the same time.

Discussion

It is obvious that cultures change over time and that historical epochs therefore need to be taken into consideration when cultural differences in socialization patterns and attachment relationships are studied. We have identified increased formal education as a driving force of generational change. Formal education is associated, in turn, with economic prosperity and differences in life histories and reproductive trajectories. Especially maternal age at first child, number of children, and household size and composition form socio-demographic milieus that are associated with cultural orientations that inform and shape child-rearing and socialization strategies. Because of the cumulative nature of such sociodemographic dimensions, it does not make sense to adopt a research strategy in which these are individually controlled (via statistical means). This point of view is the focus of controversial discussion in some segments of the scientific community (see Keller et al., 2009 and the following commentaries; Keller, 2011).

However, socio-demographic and related developmental change is only one side of the coin. Continuity and conservation are also part of historical development. As one illustration, this can be seen in the fact that cultural differences persist although historical changes are occurring – This has been demonstrated with maternal parenting behaviors in interaction with babies (e.g., Keller et al., 2005). Another arena where continuity and change can be studied is the transformation processes that migrants need to negotiate. Especially migrants coming from traditional rural contexts into Western societies are confronted with significant cultural clashes, when they need to somehow reconcile their traditional values and the new ones they face. There are findings that, with increasing formal education, behavioral norms and patterns of the new society are adopted, yet core values and behaviors are also maintained. For example, migrants from West Africa in Italy have adopted the Western middle-class distal interactional style with their babies, employing extensive face-to-face contact and ongoing conversations; yet they maintain their focus on rhythmicity in motor and vocal behavior considered crucial for Sub-Saharan rural parenting (Carra, Lavelli, Keller, & Kärtner, 2013). In theoretical terms, Kağitcibaşi (2005) had conceptualized the interplay of change and continuity that accompanies increases in formal education (also stimulated in large-scale training programs in Turkey) as the model of autonomous relatedness. As a corollary, she was one of the first to argue that the traditional relational model is not in conflict with the new autonomous model but, rather, that they can and do co-exist (see Keller, 2012).

Attachment theory and associated research has been remarkably resistant to acknowledging the cultural/historical embeddedness of psychological processes. As a recent example, after reviewing the rich diversity of child care practices around the globe, Mesman, van IJzendoorn, and Sagi-Schwartz (2016, p. 37) conclude that their investigations across different cultures are in fact 'remarkably consistent' with the claims of attachment theory, asserting that the theory stands cross-culturally validated 'until further notice' (Mesman et al., 2016, p. 37). This ignorance and resistance seems to be a characteristic of attachment theory ever since Bowlby's refusal to take Margaret Mead's cultural claims and critique seriously (Vicedo, 2017). Parallel to the view that change and continuity co-exist, and drawing on the extensive anthropological and cross-cultural literature, we argue that universality and specificity in early relationship formation co-exist. Attachment is certainly a universal human need, but how it is defined, how it evolved, and how it is deeply embedded in developmental dynamics necessarily vary across cultural contexts and changes over historical time.

Disclosure statement

No potential conflict of interest was reported by the author.

References

Ainsworth, M. D. S. (1967). *Infancy in Uganda: Infant care and the growth of love*. Baltimore, MD: Johns Hopkins University Press.

Ainsworth, M. D. S., Blehar, M. C., Waters, E., & Wall, S. (1978). *Patterns of attachment: A psychological study of the strange situation*. Hillsdale, NJ: Erlbaum.

Arnett, J. J. (2008). The neglected 95%: Why American psychology needs to become less American. *American Psychologist, 63*, 602–614.

Bernstein, B. (1971). *Class, codes and control, volume 1: Theoretical studies towards a sociology of language*. London: Routledge.

Bowlby, J. (1969). *Attachment and loss, vol. 1: Attachment*. New York, NY: Basic Books.

Bowlby, J. (1988). *A secure base: Parent-child attachment and healthy human development*. New York, NY: Basic Books.

Burkart, J. M., & van Schaik, C. P. (2010). Cognitive consequences of cooperative breeding in primates? *Animal Cognition, 13*, 1–19.

Carra, C., Lavelli, M., Keller, H., & Kärtner, J. (2013). Parenting infants: Socialization goals and behaviors of Italian mothers and immigrant mothers from West Africa. *Journal of Cross-Cultural Psychology, 44*, 1304–1320.

Cassidy, J. (2008). The nature of the child's ties. In J. Cassidy & P. R. Shaver (Eds.), *Handbook of attachment: Theory, research, and clinical applications* (2nd ed.). (pp. 3–22). New York, NY: Guilford Publications.

Chapin, B. L. (2013). Attachment in rural Sri Lanka: The shape of caregiver sensitivity, communication, and autonomy. In N. Quinn & J. M. Mageo (Eds.), *Attachment reconsidered: Cultural perspectives on a Western theory* (pp. 143–163). New York, NY: Palgrave Macmillan.

Cho, G. E., Sandel, T. L., Miller, P. M., & Wang, S.-H. (2005). What do grandmothers think about self-esteem? American and Taiwanese folk theories revisited. *Social Development, 14*, 701–721.

DuBois, C. (1944). *The people of Alor*. New York, NY: Harper and Row.

Eickhorst, A., Lamm, B., Borke, J., & Keller, H. (2008). Fatherhood in different decades: Interactions between German fathers and their infants in 1977 and 2001. *European Journal of Developmental Psychology, 5*, 92–107.

Elder, G. H., Modell, J., & Parke, R. D. (Eds.). (1993). *Children in time and place*. New York, NY: Cambridge University Press.

Fatimilehini, I., & Hassan, A. (2015). Parenting in Nigeria, contemporary families, extended family systems and religious diversity. In G. Nicolas, A. Bejarano, & D. L. Lee (Eds.), *Contemporary parenting: Global perspectives* (pp. 124–141). New York, NY: Routledge.

Greenfield, P. M. (2004). *Weaving generations together. Evolving creativity in the Maya of Chiapas*. Santa Fe, NM: Sar Press.

Gullestad, M. (1996). From obedience to negotiation: Dilemmas in the transmission of values between the generations in Norway. *The Journal of the Royal Anthropological Institute, 2*, 25–42.

Hawkes, K., O'Connell, J. F., Blurton Jones, N. G., Alvarez, H., & E. L. Charnov (2008). Grandmothering, menopause, and the evolution of human life histories. *Proceedings of the National Academy of Science of the USA, 95*, 1336–1339.

Heitmeyer, W., & Olk, T. (1995). The role of individualization theory in adolescence socialization. In G. Neubauer & H. Hurrelmann (Eds.), *Individualization in childhood and adolescence* (pp. 15–35). Berlin: de Gruyter.

Hewlett, B. S. (1991). *Intimate fathers: The nature and context of Aka Pygmy paternal infant care*. Ann Arbor: University of Michigan Press.

Kağitcibaşi, C. (2005). Autonomy and relatedness in cultural context: Implications for self and family. *Journal of Cross-Cultural Psychology, 36*, 403–422.

Keller, H. (2007). *Cultures of infancy*. Mahwah, NJ: Erlbaum.

Keller, H. (2011). Biology, culture and development: Conceptual and methodological considerations. In F. J. R. van de Vijver, A. Chasiotis, & S. Breugelmans (Eds.), *Fundamental questions in cross-cultural psychology* (pp. 312–340). Cambridge, GB: Cambridge University Press.

Keller, H. (2012). Autonomy and relatedness revisited: Cultural manifestations of universal human needs. *Child Development Perspectives, 6*, 12–18.

Keller, H., Borke, J., Staufenbiel, T., Yovsi, R. D., Abels, M., Papaligoura, Z., … Su, Y. (2009). Distal and proximal parenting as two alternative parenting strategies during infant's early months of life. A cross-cultural study. *International Journal of Behavioral Development, 33*, 412–420.

Keller, H., Borke, J., Yovsi, R. D., Lohaus, A., & Jensen, H. (2005). Cultural orientations and historical changes as predictors of parenting behaviour. *International Journal of Behavioral Development, 29*, 229–237.

Keller, H., & Chaudhary, N. (2016, April). *Is the mother essential for attachment?* Background Paper prepared for the Strüngmann Forum "Contextualizing Attachment".

Keller, H., & Demuth, C. (2005). Further explorations of the "Western mind". Mothers' and grandmothers' parental ethnotheories in Los Angels, California, and Berlin, Germany. *Forum Qualitative Social Research, 7*(1), Art. 5 (S:\TemporaryInternetFiles\Temporary Internet Files\OLK2\06-1-5-e.htm).

Keller, H., & Kärtner, J. (2013). Development – The culture-specific solution of universal developmental tasks. In M. L. Gelfand, C.-Y., Chiu, & Y. Y. Hong (Eds.), *Advances in culture and psychology* (Vol. 3, pp. 63–116). Oxford, NY: Oxford University Press.

Keller, H., & Lamm, B. (2005). Parenting as the expression of sociohistorical time. The case of German individualism. *International Journal of Behavioral Development, 29*, 238–246.

Lamm, B., Keller, H., Yovsi, R. D., & Chaudhary, N. (2008). Grandmaternal and maternal ethnotheories about early child care. *Journal of Family Psychology, 22*, 80–88.

Lamm, B., & Teiser, J. (2013). Intergenerationeller wandel. In G. Jüttemann (Ed.), *Die Entwicklungspsychologie der Menschheit* (pp. 152–163). Lengerich: Pabst Science Publishers.

Lancy, D. F. (2008). *The anthropology of childhood. Cherubs, chattel, changelings.* New York, NY: Cambridge University Press.

Marvin, R. S., Van Devender, T. I., Iwanaga, M. I., LeVine, S., & LeVine, R. A. (1977). Infant-caretaker attachment among the Hausa in Nigeria. In H. McGurk (Ed.), *Ecological factors in human development* (pp. 247–259). Amsterdam: North Holland.

Meehan, C. L., & Hawks, S. (2013). Cooperative breeding and attachment among the Aka foragers. In N. Quinn & J. Mageo (Eds.), *Attachment reconsidered: Cultural perspectives on a Western theory* (pp. 85–113). New York, NY: Palgrave.

Meins, E., Fernyhough, C., Wainwright, R., Das Gupta, M., Fradley, E., & Tuckey, M. (2002). Maternal mind-mindedness and attachment security as predictors of theory of mind understanding. *Child Development, 73*, 1715–1726.

Mesman, J., M. H. van IJzendoorn, & A. Sagi-Schwartz. (2016). Cross-cultural patterns of attachment: Universals and contextual dimensions. In J. Cassidy & P. Shaver (Eds.), *Handbook of attachment* (3rd ed., pp. 790–815). New York, NY: Guilford.

Minde, K., Corter, C., Goldberg, S., & Jeffers, D. (1990). Maternal preference between premature twins up to age four. *Journal of the American Academy of Child and Adolescent Psychiatry, 29*, 367–374.

Mjelde-Mossey, L. A. (2007). Cultural and demographic changes and their effects upon the traditional grandparent role for chinese elders. *Journal of Human Behavior in Social Environment, 16*, 107–120.

Morelli, G. (2015). The evolution of attachment theory and cultures of human attachment in infancy and early childhood. In L. A. Jensen (Ed.), *The Oxford handbook of human development and culture* (pp. 149–164). New York, NY: Oxford University Press.

Sabatier, C., & Lannegrand-Willem, L. (2005). Transmission of family values and attachment: A French three-generation study. *Applied Psychology: An International Review, 54*, 378–395.

Saraswathi, T. S., & Pai, S. (1997). Socialization in the Indian context. In H. S. R. Kao & D. Sinha (Eds.), *Asian perspectives on psychology* (pp. 74–92). New Dehli: Sage.

Scheidecker, G. (2014). *"Fürchte den Zorn deiner Ahnen!" Zur Sozialisation moralischer Emotionen im Süden Madagaskars* ["Be afraid of the revenge of your ancestors Socialisation of moral emotions in the South of Madagaskar]" (Dissertation). Fachbereich Politik- und Sozialwissenschaften, Freie Universitat Berlin.

Schröder, L., Keller, H., & Kleis, A. (2013). Parent-child conversations in three urban middle-class contexts: Mothers and fathers reminisce with their daughters and sons in Costa Rica, Mexico, and Germany. *Actualidades en Psicologia, 27*, 81–104.

Sever, L. (1989). Change in women's perceptions of parental child rearing attitudes in Turkey: A three generation comparison. *Early Child Development and Care, 50*, 131–138. doi:10.1080/0300443890500111

Sünker, H. (1995). Childhood between individualization and institutionalization. In G. Neubauer & H. Hurrelmann (Eds.), *Individualization in childhood and adolescence* (pp. 37–51). Berlin: de Gruyter.

Tronick, E. Z., Morelli, G. A., & Winn, S. (1987). Multiple caretaking of Efe (Pygmy) infants. *American Anthropologist, 89*, 96–106.

Vicedo, M. (2013). *The nature and nurture of love. From imprinting to attachment in cold war America*. Chicago: University of Chicago Press.

Vicedo, M. (2017). Putting attachment in its place: Disciplinary and cultural contexts. *European Journal of Developmental Psychology*. Retrieved from http://www.tandfonline.com/doi/full/10.1080/17405629.2017.1289838

Voland, E., Chasiotis, A., & Schiefenhövel, W. (2004). Das Paradox der zweiten Lebenshälfte: Warum gibt es Großmütter? *Biologie in unserer Zeit, 6*, 366–370.

Xie, X., & Xia, Y. (2011). Grandparenting in Chinese immigrant families. *Marriage and Family Review, 47*, 383–396. doi:10.1080/01494929.2011.594218

Authority, disciplinary intimacy & parenting in middle-class America

Stephen Lassonde

ABSTRACT
Children learn about authority first from their parents. A shift in orientation to authority occurred during middle-class formation in the mid-nineteenth century U.S., a style of parenting described as 'disciplinary intimacy.' A century later disciplinary intimacy, or 'child-centered' parenting characterized childrearing advice across American society. Simultaneously, distrust of all institutions in the liberal democratic state accelerated, causing questioning and confusion at every level of society. In family life, disciplinary practices once considered necessary, such as corporal punishment, came to be regarded as harsh and responsible for authoritarianism. Child-centered parenting, while discouraging 'restrictive' childrearing practices, gave little direction about constructive correctives, which fueled parental anxiety even as developmentalists temporarily resolved the decades-long controversy about restrictive vs. 'permissive' parenting. By the 1990s a debate formerly contrasting working- and middle-class childrearing values was overshadowed by a second shift focused on children's school success as earlier considerations of authority and discipline faded from view. As concern spreads about the rise of authoritarianism across the West, the politics of parenting may once again preoccupy social scientists who worry about the nascence of sectarianism, xenophobia, and bellicose nationalism.

1. Introduction

Between 1950 and 1975 virtually every institution in American life was roiled by challenges to the public's faith in its ability to uphold its purpose. Family life, religion, schooling, the military, law enforcement, democratic rule, and civic life were all scrutinized as never before. Assumptions that underlay fundamental understandings of race, gender, sexuality, and social status were contested. Few of these assumptions remained unchanged; few institutions untested. In fact, no organization that took a hand in forming young people's ideas about right and wrong, fact and fiction, consent and privilege, trust and skepticism, loyalty and dissent was left untouched. The building blocks of the developing child's trust in authority – obedience, respect, conformity, and faith – were dissolved and never quite recast (Heclo, 2008; Marwick, 1998).

Baby Boom children, in other words, grew up in an era of deepening doubt about, or disenchantment with, authority as soon as they could walk: in rapid succession, the unraveling of McCarthyism and deepening Cold War during the early to mid-1950s was followed by the resurgence of the Civil Rights Movement. The launching of the Sputnik satellite by the Soviet Union in 1957 provoked an unending crisis in American education. Soon after, outgoing U.S. president and former World War Two hero Dwight Eisenhower warned about the dangers of unmonitored complicity between the nation's military and its private enterprise. The assassinations of the Kennedy brothers and Martin Luther King, Jr., in the next decade, shook the democratic process to its core. By the latter half of the 1960s resistance to the military draft and mass protest against U.S. involvement in the Vietnam war occurred against the backdrop of a sexual revolution, the celebration of youth culture, and the recognition of a widening ideological divide between parents and their children. The Women's Movement and the Gay Rights Movement in the late-1960s and early-1970s exposed the injustices of patriarchy and heteronormativity. The political scandals of Watergate and its aftermath seemed to confirm Americans' worst fears that, at the highest levels, democracy was corroded by greed and corruption. Suspicion and cynicism about the legitimacy of all forms of authority left public trust in tatters. 'Question Authority,' the slogan championed by counter-culture father figure Timothy Leary, became the anthem of the generation coming of age in the 1960s and 1970s.

Preceding all of these upheavals, however, as early as the 1930s, among a newly-influential group of 'scientific' childrearing experts, there was a dawning reorientation of family relations in the United States that promoted parity (between parents and children and husbands and wives) over the asymmetry of inheritance, privilege, and patriarchy. This modulation of tone, and a new stress on democracy in family decision-making and parent-child interaction, reverberated through the following decades, finding full expression in the 1960s. In tandem with the spread of what came to be called 'child-centered' parenting, the feminist insight at the end of the 1960s that 'the personal is political' collapsed previously well-patrolled distinctions between public and private life, exposing the constructs of power in intimate relations that refracted through the political economy of Western capitalism (Hanisch, 1970). The contraceptive revolution of the 1960s, the rise of feminism and of women's reproductive rights, the movement toward zero population growth by 1970, and the widespread adoption of no-fault divorce all helped to accelerate the push for the democratization of family life. The presumptions of all types of male domination formed a through-line from the bedroom to the boardroom. The prerogative of the male breadwinner, laws that treated women as the financial dependents of their spouses, economic inequities in the marketplace and in the household, and the absence of women's representation in political office came to be seen as nested and mutually reinforcing.

The advocacy of a more democratic family structure by psychologists before World War Two seemed to portend a more equitable, just society. No one could have predicted the dissolution of trust that followed instead. Social theorists like Theodor Adorno and the social psychologists who collaborated with him to produce *The Authoritarian Personality* concluded that forceful fathers and cowering children had prepared the way for Hitler and totalitarianism the world over. Indeed, they speculated that parenting styles that downplayed obedience and encouraged independent thinking might inoculate Americans against the kind of political cataclysm that had led to the rise of fascism and world war. *The Authoritarian Personality* claimed that parents who scored low on the study's 'bias scale' were more egalitarian, placed less stress on obedience, and were more tolerant of their children's behavior, even when it veered into the 'socially unacceptable.' They raised children who were 'more accepting of people different than themselves,' confident about articulating their differences with others and with their parents, and 'more comfortable challenging authority' (Adorno, Frenkel-Brunswick, Levinson, & Sanford, 1969, p. 387).

Flaws in the study's methodology and the shadow cast over it by McCarthyism quickly drained the study of influence. However, one of the survey's conclusions continued to resonate with childrearing experts. The implied relationship between childrearing practices and political persuasion by the authors of *The Authoritarian Personality* would shape the 'synthesis' of developmentalists who strived to reconcile the restrictiveness of pre-World War Two Behaviorism with what came to be thought of as 'child-centered' parenting. What is more, the wisdom of developmentalists' claims about the egalitarian ethos of middle-class parenting appears, in retrospect, to have been prescient about the coming crisis of authority across the spectrum of American institutional life. Skepticism of authority in the rising generation clashed with political reactions to the challenges of the Civil Rights, antiwar, and other social movements. Although inspired by an intellectual tradition distinct from second-wave feminism, Adorno's anchoring of political attitudes in family life, at its core, shared the future feminist insight into the domestic bases of political economy. Pivotal here, then, is not the methodological soundness of the study's findings but rather its sharing the belief that attitudes cultivated in the daily practices of the American family had political ramifications (Jones & Cox, 2012).

2. Paternal authority & human capital

Of all the ways that children learn about authority, the most immediate, germinal, and continuous are acquired in the bosom of the family.It is in the context of family relations that children learn their first, most important lessons about the relationship of self to others: self-regard, reciprocity, trust, the nature of their commitments to others, and the role of adults in their lives are all grounded in the family experience (Vicedo, 2013). It is within the social membrane of the family sphere that the child first encounters the idea of authority. In the family the child learns to comply with and resist the wishes of parents and siblings, and first encounters the rewards and punishments of obedience and rebellion. If it is the parents' ultimate aim to teach the child to crave independence, the cultivation of autonomy is rooted, paradoxically, in the infant's dependency on parental beneficence: nutrition, shelter, affection, praise, hygiene, and pleasure. The psychologically healthy child gradually finds ways to satisfy each of these needs on its own or in reciprocity with non-family members, on the path to adulthood.

As 'natural' as the parents' authority may appear in the eyes of the growing child, the demands of the world outside the home are actively normalized by parents, ideally, through their interactions with others, and with adults in particular. Both by example and through explicit instruction, parents show children how to conduct themselves with non-family members in the most sensible and frictionless manner. While mothers have played a primary and holistic role in framing children's interactions with non-familial others, fathers, according to historians, also served this function explicitly and symbolically, 'translating' the 'utilitarian' aspect of authority to the child's understanding of its relationship to those outside the household. While they socialized the child's encounters with non-family members, fathers also personified for the child the inherent coercive capacity that exists in this, the most intimate of superior-subordinate relationships. Fathers possessed and periodically exercised the physical power to enforce their will on their children from infancy to adulthood.

Although historians have documented the retreat of fathers from child nurture since the early nineteenth century, in the recent past, developmentalists have reflected on contemporary fathers' contributions to children's material development (i.e., their economic resources such as cash, property, tools, etc.), and also children's development of social and cultural capital. Although more circumscribed than in the past, fathers still perform as critical mediators between their children's encounters with, and understanding of, authority (Milkie & Denny, 2013; Pleck, 2007). Before the industrial age fathers taught children practical skills that prepared them for vocations. In colonial America fathers were the spiritual leaders of the Protestant household – 'a little commonwealth' – and the guarantors of children's Christian learning (Demos, 1970, 1982, pp. 425–445; Hill, 1964; Ryan, 1981). As long as the household remained the site of production, as it did through the early decades of the nineteenth century, the image of father as active patriarch was credible. And while mothers bore the brunt of daily care-giving for the very young in early America, parenting had the semblance of a partnership, with father as the legal, moral, and symbolic head of family.

In John Demos's portrait, the father in early New England loomed large in the lives of his children. Demos ticks off his many roles: 'progenitor,' 'psychologist,' 'pedagogue,' (role) 'model,' 'caregiver,' 'companion,' 'teacher,' 'benefactor,' 'moral overseer,' and 'guidance counselor' (Demos, 1982, pp. 458–464).

Still, even though their role in the daily responsibilities of childrearing receded, fathers continued to model how to behave toward people in the concentric circles of their orbit, such as neighbors, clergy, teachers, functionaries of every kind, shopkeepers, clerks, bosses, and of course the police and others responsible for upholding civic authority. Fathers, in other words, imparted every form of 'capital' that shaped the child's destiny. While contemporary developmentalists don't often include 'human capital' in their inventory of skills developed by fathers in their children, Demos argues persuasively that before the era of mass schooling fathers were fully engaged in their children's cultivation of life skills and other attributes that contributed to their competence as future adults. The practice of 'putting out' children to other households in early New England, for instance, was a way of enhancing family resources while simultaneously training a child in a skill or trade (Demos, 1970; Morgan, 1944). The concept of human capital was coined by economist Gary Becker (1980) to describe *all* the ways that a young person acquires the means to make a living, and includes what Pierre Bourdieu and Passeron (1990) would describe as traits, habits, dispositions, linguistic facility, literacy, social connections, and access to power or influence that enhances or secures the child's social standing.

3. The feminization of discipline

As capitalism stimulated the concentration of population in cities during the early nineteenth century, as it fueled industrialization and revolutions in energy use, the extraction of raw materials, productivity, transportation, communication, and the distribution of goods, the household no longer functioned as the locus of production but of reproduction. This process intensified the gendered division of labor, externalizing work for cash and domesticating most forms of unpaid labor, including the care and feeding of children and other household members. In the nascent urban middle class, the division of labor and encouragement of role-specialization along gender lines was most advanced and cultivated women's orientation to the emotional sustenance of family members above all other callings. As the bases of fathers' authority began to shrink, mothers' responsibility for developing capacities in their children that would enable them to conduct themselves successfully in the world beyond the household – to live independently and, ultimately, to form families of their own – grew. In the process of shouldering most aspects of child nurture, mothers promoted another change: rather than relying primarily on the child's fear of the consequences of wrongdoing or ill behavior, mothers placed greater emphasis on engendering 'self' control in children.

In her book on the rise of the middle-class family in mid-nineteenth century America, Mary P. Ryan describes the aim of successful childrearing as the installation of a 'portable parent' in the mind of the child. Ryan's portable parent firmly conveys the idea of a child who has fully internalized its mother's voice (Ryan, 1981). Literary historian Richard H. Brodhead subsequently named this nascent theory of child socialization 'disciplinary intimacy.' Disciplinary intimacy banished corporal punishment, enshrined parental restraint, and secured children's compliance by changing the foundations of the child's understanding of authority. Instead of colonizing the child, disciplinary intimacy suggests something closer to Pierre Bourdieu's 'disposition,' which describes a relationship in which the child actively participates in its direction by the parent – is *inclined* to do as the parent wishes, because it is disposed to (Burawoy, 2012). Brodhead's pithy analysis captures the subtlety of its psychological technique:

> [E]nmeshing the child in strong bonds of love is the way authority introduces its charge to its imperatives and norms ... In later development the child's continuing direction of itself toward its parents' warmth and favor – the disposition this whole plan of nurture exists to intensify and to transform from a primal instinct into the ground of the child's emerging selfhood – establishes an agency, within the child's nature, enforcing the feeling of obligation to parentally embodied values. (Brodhead, 1988)

Brodhead's characterization of an emergent affective style is derived from myriad sources of mid-nineteenth century American middle-class culture: mass-market fiction, religious tracts, women's, family, and children's magazines, and advice to mothers by self-proclaimed male and female authorities on the subject (Baym, 1978; Davidson, 1986; Douglas, 1977; Sklar, 1973; Tompkins, 1985).

Authority, as Brodhead demonstrates exhaustively, was the issue at the center of all of these and as James Block has since observed, it was the appearance of the child's complicity in its conscious restraint, its seeming willingness to yield to the parent's authority (compliance without complaint) that defined this new mode of child nurture (Block, 2012). The chasm between the *appearance* of children's supposed volition-to comply or not-and the consequences of non-compliance, the withdrawal of parental approval (love), was of course at the root of confusion from the very introduction of the new method. Formerly obedience had been based in the Puritanical fear of outright rejection, physical punishment, and even eternal damnation, but now it yielded to a more nebulous insistence on the *performance* of obedience. This framework was the foundation for child-centered parenting a century later and as we will see, created for parents aspiring to adopt the habits and bearing of middle-class culture, a style of discipline that rejected physical punishment and shaming in favor of affection and praise. Awareness of child-centered parenting, popularized by Dr Benjamin Spock, registered well beyond the middle-class audience that had been its intended target up to World War Two, even while the breadth of its actual practice is less clear (Strickland & Ambrose, 1985). What is certain is that corporal punishment lingered long after it was legally proscribed and publicly frowned upon. And for parents at mid-century – parents of the Baby Boom – acceptance or rejection of this disciplinary binary came to define their social standing in the eyes of new experts who championed the science of childrearing.

Significantly, for the looming importance of debates over 'school readiness' by the end of the twentieth century, corporal punishment was the least dependent on language to deploy or for the child to understand. It was the most direct and communicative of the parents' means to control the behavior of the youngest of children – those most animalistic in their preverbal condition. In such moments the parent's sheer exercise of power overshadowed every mechanism shy of physical redress, as the entire spectrum from reward for good behavior to the withdrawal of affection and denial of privilege was suspended. The 'soft power' of persuasion through disapproving glances and words is eclipsed by the parent's ability to inflict physical suffering. Think here of the difference between 'co-optive power' (the ability to 'shape preferences'), which is the favored method of disciplinary intimacy, and what Joseph Nye calls 'coercive,' or 'hard-power,' which is the ability to simply tell others what to do (Nye, 1990). To be subjected to physical punishment was to be treated as the most senseless kind of human being and, so, to be shamed even as shaming receded as a preferred method of correction. Even with restrictive parenting in abeyance, then, the child didn't become insensible to fear, shame, guilt, and physical punishment but, on the contrary, became hypersensitive to their implementation.

At bottom, parental authority is realized through parents' ability to feed, clothe, shelter, and (by the late twentieth century) educate their children. Traditionally the law has enforced that authority, the baldest expression of which was once the power of the parent to impose his or her will on the child by the ability to inflict pain and even death (Shurtleff, 1853). Disciplinary intimacy effectively shifted the threat of violence explicit in the old disciplinary mode to the threat of alienated affection – from physical pain to emotional pain.

The love temporarily withdrawn, however, was mostly mother's love. Father, in the new economic order that arose with the growth of cities and the spread of industrialization, was absent for most of each day and, more important, often emotionally remote in any case. The key phrase in Brodhead's description of disciplinary intimacy, which asserts that its effect is to establish 'an agency *within* the child's nature' (my emphasis), turns upon the mother's effectiveness at inculcating a desire in the child to seek mother's approval. The child's progress on the path to self-control is manifested by its willingness to exercise agency over itself. Over time this self-mastery results in the child's autonomy and, ultimately, maturity and adulthood. With the rise of disciplinary intimacy, then, self-control became the guiding goal of middle-class child nurture, even as debates ensued about the best means of helping the child attain it.

The rising visibility of mothers as children's exclusive caretakers coincided with a century-long movement in middle-class parenting from an attitude of restrictiveness to permissiveness (Ryan, 1981; Stearns, 2003). Driving this change, according to historian Peter Stearns, was an underlying conception of the child that morphed from the resilient and 'sturdy' child into the twentieth century's 'vulnerable child,' who lacked resiliency. By the mid-twentieth century, one of the consequences of the new view of children was profound confusion among parents about what positive mandates guided the more permissive posture. More commonly, Stearns says, it was clear what *not* to do – physical punishment, fear, guilt, and shame, the four pillars of nineteenth-century parenting were out – but what replaced them? Postwar childrearing had promised life-long satisfactions to parents, but according to Stearns, it became instead a well of anxiety: parents had to weigh every stricture against the fear of emotionally scarring their children.

In place of the decisiveness and clarity that had characterized parenting up to the middle decades of the twentieth century, permissive parenting required a parent to engage in enormously time-consuming discussions with each child about the rationale behind every prohibition. Stearns has hit upon something extremely important in pointing to the salience of parental anxiety across the course of the twentieth century. In the post-World War Two era parents began to suffer from a confusion of means in child discipline. Uncertainty about how to replace what 'not to do' with what they *should* be doing overwhelmed parents, Stearns shows, fueling a gnawing worry about how to raise their children.

Parents' anxiety about how to raise their children arose not only from a confusion of means (the movement from restrictive to permissive disciplinary styles over the course of a century) but a confusion of ends: how to foster autonomy in children while exercising control over them at the same time. But this, as we shall see, is primarily a middle-class concern. Since the end of the Baby Boom, parents' preoccupations shifted and bifurcated. For middle-class parents, the goal of engendering autonomy in children and launching them into adulthood remained an important developmental milestone, but it has been progressively deferred and sublimated to the more pressing issue of enabling their adult children to grow into future middle-class selves.

For working-class children independence was never really a question developmentally. The establishment of mass schooling by the beginning of the twentieth century had reversed the ancient dependence of parents on children. Schooling institutionalized children's dependence on parents in unaccustomed ways. It upset the prevailing sense of intergenerational reciprocity and the presumption of the child's ability to contribute to the household economy at an early age. But the goal of fostering the child's financial independence and ability one day to contribute his or her rightful share of earnings to the family economy remained entrenched at least through World War Two (Lassonde, 2005; Warner & Srole, 1945).

Here, however, it is important to draw attention, if briefly, to an aspect of children's socialization during the twentieth century that, until the publication of Paula Fass's, *The End of American Childhood* (2016), has largely escaped the notice of historians of childhood. American family sociologists and social workers were deeply interested in the generational tension that surfaced when immigrant children entered high school before World War Two. But as Fass so vividly demonstrates, scores of memoirs about the period document innumerable personal variations on the often-violent clashes that could characterize relations between immigrant parents and their adolescent children during these years.

Early in the century, before high school had become a mass institution sociologists and social workers frequently commented upon the variety of ethnic twists on 'American' vs. 'foreign-born' attitudes toward authority in parent-child relations. The rigidity of 'Old World Traits Transplanted' was contrasted with the 'healthier,' laissez-faire tendencies of American parenting. As high school became commonplace, it forced this generational battle to the surface of American life. Parental authority was everywhere on the run and schooling offered, for most immigrant working-class adolescents, a mode of relating to parents, adults, and to authority figures in general, starkly at odds with what their parents demanded at home. Moreover, in a foreshadowing of economic changes by the century's end, children's tendency to look to parents for vocational guidance receded with the rapid rise of white collar occupations before and after World War Two.

Intensifying this drift, as lingual and cultural 'natives' children overmatched their parents whenever they set foot outside their parents' homes. (Bailyn, 1960; Graebner, 1990). Immigrant parental authority seems to have existed, increasingly, in name only, or alternatively (and tragically), as an exaggerated and permanently alienating assertion of parents' desire to control every aspect the adolescent's developing personal and social life. For the most part, this dimension of Americans' orientation to authority and child development during the middle of the twentieth century is utterly absent from the narrative of child-rearing experts. Significantly, this vein of sociological inquiry, so prominent during the first half of the twentieth century, evaporated from sociological discourse by midcentury (Lynd & Lynd, 1929, 1937; Centers, 1950; Bronfenbrenner, 1958). This is attributable to a combination of influences, including the cessation of mass immigration after 1924, the trend toward intra-religion intermarriage (the so-called 'triple melting pot'), the work of the high schools to Americanize teens, and of course, the nationalism of World War Two. As their research became more and more attuned to youths' socioeconomic differences after World War Two, the explanatory power of ethnicity, it appears, began to fade into the background of American social science (Warner & Srole, pp. 103–155).

4. Child-centered parenting & social status

Histories of childrearing in the second half of the twentieth century have been of two kinds. One provides a retrospective summary of the field by researchers in child development. A second kind, written by historians, analyzes trends in the use of expert childrearing advice by developmentalists and their popularizers. In 1993 developmentalist Eleanor E. Maccoby produced an incisive overview of themes in child socialization that traced the early influences of Freudian psychoanalysis and of Behaviorism. The impact of child socialization research on parenting practices in her account is but a feature of a much larger canvas of competing theories driving research on children's socialization during the twentieth century (Maccoby, 1992). These studies document what parents believed and did and stand in stark contrast to what childrearing advice prescribed. It is worth accounting for, for that reason alone, but it also offers more direct information about parents' views of authority and its role in children's lives during this critical period.

In what would become a classic in the literature on childrearing and socioeconomic status, developmentalist Urie Bronfenbrenner showed that at midcentury the disciplinary practices of middle-class and working-class parents were moving in opposite directions (Bronfenbrenner, 1958). Working-class parenting, previously deemed more permissive in all areas of childrearing than middle-class parenting, was becoming more restrictive than it had been a generation earlier, and middle-class parenting, restrictive in the years between 1930 and the end of World War Two, was relaxing. Developmentalists during the second half of the twentieth century were confounded by the direction and pace of change in each group. The apogee of permissiveness, it seems, was reached just as the Baby Boom peaked. Spock's 1957 edition of *Baby and Child Care* counseled parents for the first time to firm up their discipline if they wanted children to be both happy and well-behaved (Bronfenbrenner, 1958, p. 423). One outcome in the long term, though by no means certain, In Bronfenbrenner's assessment, was that working- and middle- class parents' disciplinary styles might converge. What was certain, he said, is that 'socialization practices seem most likely to be altered in those segments of society which have readiest access to the agencies or agents of change (e.g., books, pamphlets, physicians, and counselors)' (Bronfenbrenner, 1958, p. 424). Most striking however was Bronfenbrenner's caution to middle-class parents, whose 'high levels of expectations for ultimate performance' by their children seemed at odds with their more relaxed attitude toward discipline. The resulting disconnect between permissive parenting and high expectations, he speculated, suggested that 'days of disappointment lay ahead for middle-class fathers and mothers' (Bronfenbrenner, 1958, p. 415).

While none of the studies cited by Bronfenbrenner explicitly addressed the degree to which parenting styles of middle- and working-class Americans revealed or rejected authoritarian values, for two important studies published a decade later (Baumrind, 1966; Kohn, 1969), *The Authoritarian Personality* hummed loudly in the background. By this time, corporal punishment had become a cultural marker and litmus test for enlightened parenting. Its discouragement was an index of cultural capital and its use registered impoverishment in this arena: an absence of the capacity to gain access to potentially invaluable resources for self-promotion, accomplishment, and success. Corporal punishment had become a stand-in for class distinction at a time when industrial occupations were beginning to evaporate and the future of working-class Americans seemed destined to wither on the vine (Rubin, 1976).

In *Class and Conformity* (1969) sociologist Melvin L. Kohn sought to understand the complex interrelationships of childrearing, gender, education, occupation, an inclination to conform or the ability to think flexibly. Kohn critiqued previous studies as overly focused on the comparative likelihood of parents' use of physical vs. psychological/emotional sanctioning of misbehavior by social class. More important for Kohn than *which* form of punishment was employed by a parent was the 'when and the why' a parent would employ one kind of discipline over another (Kohn, 1969). Middle-class parents were less likely to use physical punishment not because they were more interested in long-term behavioral goals as compared with working-class parents, but because they feared that punishing overt misbehavior might inhibit their children's expressiveness and independent thinking. Middle-class occupations rewarded these attributes, according to Kohn, and allowed a worker to be 'self-directed.' Flexible thinking made possible self-directed work and self-directed work in turn encouraged flexible thinking.

Working-class men, by contrast, he concluded, valued conformity and lacked self-direction. The main thrust of Kohn's study was to determine whether this was due to limits imposed by the nature of their occupations or whether the content and level of their education had limited their capacity to think flexibly. Childrearing, though secondary to these variables, was related to values that either fostered or discouraged mental flexibility, in Kohn's analysis. Kohn's main finding here was that physical punishment was used somewhat more by working-class parents than middle-class parents, but more meaningful was that middle-class parents dispensed physical punishment depending on their perception of the child's intentions. Working-class parents punished children simply for flouting accepted norms. The focus on intent, Kohn suggested, reinforced habits of flexible thinking which were also nurtured by educational success, while punishment of overt transgressions reinforced the importance of conformity, which discourages flexible thinking. In the end, he concluded that the work experiences of laborers rather than education itself had the greater effect on self-directed behavior. And while the issue of physical punishment played a secondary role in his analysis, his attempt to deconstruct corporal punishment implicated childrearing in the particular forms of human capital that working-class and middle-class parents each hoped to cultivate in their children.

Occupational success for working-class men was determined by a number of attributes including the willingness to acknowledge a hierarchy based on skill and aptitude, a willingness to take direction, and to subordinate one's own desires to those of the group and its goals. 'Conformity' is a fraught word in American political discourse. It is the opposite of independence, self-fulfillment, and traditional American conceptions of masculinity. So its choice by Kohn is curious, since his aim was to explain, non-judgmentally, the differing perspectives of working-class parents compared with their middle-class contemporaries. But what he also tries to show is how the demand for conformity by working-class parents was connected to, and promoted the development of, a capacity for human capital in ways consistent with working-class occupational success. To learn the skills of a worker one needs to listen, to emulate, and to cooperate. One needs patience and to comprehend the benchmarks of success that mark the path of occupational progress, just as 'expressiveness,' 'self-control,' and 'independent thinking' are crucial to educational progress, future stability, and success in middle-class occupations.

As restrictive and permissive parenting continued to be studied by developmentalists, by the mid-1960s Dr Spock remained the sole, recognizable voice in American childrearing. The political context of childrearing and its role in citizens' views of authority, however, was transformed during that volatile decade. Spock, despite having modified his views, came under fire for promoting a style of parenting that would be blamed for the radicalization of U.S. youth, for inspiring protest against the Vietnam War, and spawning a youth counterculture, including dangerous experimentation with recreational drugs (Hulbert, 2003). It was against this background of confusion, disappointment, and rising cynicism that the debate between restrictiveness and permissiveness came to a resting place. In the midst of the controversy about American parenting styles, psychologist Diana Baumrind's corrective emerged. Baumrind's prescriptions for what she called 'authoritative' parenting split the difference between presumed authoritarian tendencies attributed to Watsonian Behaviorism and Spock's (and others') reputed permissiveness. She framed her synthesis in 1966 as a reply to the 'pejorative' effects of *The Authoritative Personality* on the understanding of authority in American life, urging an agnostic interpretation of the concept and a reining-in of parental permissiveness as necessary for children's developing sense of competence. In short, she argued that it was time to abandon the 'either/or' view of parenting as nurturance vs. control, 'combining responsiveness' (a more neutral term than 'permissiveness') … and 'demandingness' (which was a less-loaded term than 'authoritarian') … 'rather than choosing one over the other' (Baumrind, 1966; Criss & Larzelere, 2013, p. 3). Baumrind's work sought to reduce the confusion that 'child-centered' parenting had introduced with its emphasis on 'don'ts over 'dos' (Baumrind, 1971). In time, Baumrind herself was criticized for her seeming blindness to the importance of differences in cultural receptivity to restrictive disciplinary practices. Chinese immigrant children in the

U.S., it was shown, for instance, suffered none of the ill effects of 'authoritarian' parenting because the context of its delivery to and absorption by children had a positive, mitigating impact (Chao, 1994). But the overall effect of Baumrind's synthesis for decades was a stabilizing adjustment that at least addressed the deepening confusion (and anxiety) manifest among middle-class parents until they were renewed and extended by social trends enacted by Baby Boomers as they themselves entered parenthood.

5. Discipline, human capital & school performance

With the retreat of the 1960s, political and social upheaval died down even as authority was challenged in every corner of American life. And while contrasts between middle- and working-class childrearing practices remained, the use and tolerance of physical punishment declined at the same time. As the U.S. economy endured a corrosive, decades-long decline in good-paying, dependable, long-term industrial jobs from the 1960s forward, working-class Americans morphed in the political vernacular into 'working Americans.' This change, it seems, sought to erase distinctions between the working class and middle-class Americans, as it became increasingly popular to defend the interests of the middle class at the expense, especially, of the working poor. But it also betrayed growing discomfort with belonging to a category of people who made a living by working with their hands. To be working class was to 'fail' somehow, personally, socially, and occupationally. While it is a commonplace to say that in the United States everyone aspires to be, and calls him- or herself 'middle class,' beneath this is the perception that working-class Americans are those being left behind in a post-industrial economy (Isenberg, 2016). In the twenty-first century in the United States, disinterest in or failure at school leads to almost certain marginalization in the marketplace or, at best, a work life destined to be foreshortened by occupational obsolescence or the gradual incapacitation of age and infirmity (Brooks, 2016). Because of this, much of the work on childrearing and human capital since the end of the twentieth century has focused almost exclusively on school-aged children. Except in the specific context of the 'school-readiness' debate, which currently revolves around the 'word gap' that emerges from birth to school age, the historical and social science literature has largely overlooked parents' part in shaping children's attitudes about authority and its role in cultivating children's life skills (Zelizer, 2005; Hart & Risley, 1995; Kessen, 1966).

As worries about the political consequences of parenting faded, the implications of working-class compared with middle-class childrearing practices eventually moved on to other concerns (Calarco, 2014). By the 1990s the authoritarian/permissive binary was replaced by heightened attention to the relationship between parenting styles and school success. In the emerging hierarchy of societal authority, education (the child's ability to master her- or himself, after all, was the enduring feature of school success) displaced parental disciplinary style as evidence that the child was properly raised (Grant, 2014). Physical correction, verbal humiliation, parental stridency, became vestiges of a style of authority that had slipped over the horizon. Quietly, the most damning thing about such behavior was less what it said about the latent authoritarian impulses of the parent than what it predicted about the child's *future* financial trajectory. Recall, in Kohn's attempt to understand the values informing middle-class and working-class attitudes toward discipline and authority, success in school was, for middle-class parents, a value that accompanied their goals of inculcating flexible thinking, expressiveness, self-control, and autonomy. In Kohn's analysis, childrearing, education, and ultimately occupation formed, then consolidated, an orientation toward autonomy or conformity, but a generation later, education became an end in itself. All other socially-defining experiences either supported or undermined it. (Fordham & Ogbu, 1986).

By the 1980s, echoes of disciplinary intimacy could be heard in reconsiderations of measures of intelligence and in the compatibility of capacities developed in preschoolers with future school success. Famously, developmentalist Howard Gardner (1983) and somewhat later social psychologists Peter Salovey and John D. Mayer (1989) identified, essentially, the underlying 'science' of 'multiple intelligences' and then more specifically of 'emotional intelligence' in mental health and socially adaptive behavior. Salovey and Mayer defined emotional intelligence as 'the subset of social intelligence that involves the ability to monitor one's own and others' feelings and emotions, to discriminate among them and to use this information to guide one's thinking and actions' (Salovey & Mayer, 1989). Earlier in the same decade, sociologist Arlie Russell Hochschild highlighted a connection between the type of 'emotional work' demanded by pink and white collar jobs, which leaned heavily upon the very qualities nurtured in the child-centered family and which in fact supported the prodigious growth of the service sector in the U.S. economy during the second half of the twentieth century (Hochschild, 1983).

A generation later, it has become increasingly doubtful whether the psychological techniques of disciplinary intimacy can launch autonomous young adults into the world beyond the range of parental influence. With the breathtaking commodification of college rankings in the United States, the escalation of college tuition over the last two decades, and the rising numbers of 18–34 year-olds returning to live with parents before marriage, the demography of independence certainly challenges the presumption that adulthood can be attained even very soon after the achievement of a college degree (Pew Research Center, 2016). Rising levels of educational attainment and the corresponding upward creep of age-at-first-marriage demonstrate that the expectation that a young person would any longer reach adulthood in his or her early twenties ended with the generation that spawned the baby boom. Baby Boomers themselves extended adolescence well into their twenties but their children, millennials, have postponed marriage and adulthood even further, so that sociologists of the life cycle have created a new category of human development, which they call 'emerging adulthood' (Arnett, 2000; Fry, 2015).

The accretion of yet another stage of development in preparation for adulthood reflects the degree to which the timing of children's maturity is out of step with contemporary child-nurture. This is due in part to its origin in the historical formation of the middle class, an incipient culture born of the 'separate spheres' ideology that declared women's purpose and domain to be the physical, spiritual, and emotional functioning of the household. Within this sphere the key ideas of childrearing – the cultivation of children's development and independence – were forged by women during the early decades of the nineteenth century. The demography of emerging adulthood in the current century, however, the ideology of disciplinary intimacy, the obsolescence of fathers as the progenitors of human capital, and the desire to create a world in which women and men are true equals may be at odds with the attainment of the traditional accoutrements of adulthood. As we try to accommodate delayed entry into adult independence and childrearing practices that, in Bronfenbrenner's assessment, are more forgiving and situational than in the past but still insist on a prescribed level of achievement from children as they age, Bronfenbrenner's prediction that 'days of disappointment lay ahead' resonate with the mounting anxiety of parents in fear of 'letting go' of their adult children.

Historians have highlighted one of the more nuanced, least discussed aspects of these disjunctions: As adolescents face the prospect of growing into adulthood, they labor under a persistent adult-like regimen that is often perceived as necessary to future success (Brooks, 2001; Chua, 2011; Wihbey, 2011). These demands, however, can be at odds with the goal of fostering their autonomy. For while the attainment of maturity for one's children remains the ultimate goal for parents, its arrival has been late in coming because of a reluctance by parents to relinquish control of decision-making for their children as they approach chronological adulthood (Fass, 2016; Fass & Grossberg, 2012; Pew Research Center, 2016). It is little wonder then, as Stearns has shown, that middle-class parents have become more anxious with each passing decade. In an era of diminishing faith in every institution that sustained most aspects of a liberal democratic society, one is tempted to observe that parents' confusion about how to raise competent, successful children has been wholly consistent with their experience in every other realm of American life.

During the mid-twentieth century, the sequence and timing of entry into adulthood enjoyed a brief phase of faithful enactment by the majority of young women and men. Adulthood by one's early twenties seemed a certainty for most Americans (Modell, 1989). It was also a time when success in school was still but one of a several paths to financial and social autonomy. Educational attainment, more than any other factor, caused young people to delay their ultimate achievement of financial and other markers of independence (Modell, 1989). Yet, from another perspective, at stake in the failure to shift from the old disciplinary regime to child-centered parenting were worrisome political dispositions that for some, had explained the catastrophic plunge into world war during the twentieth century. After the 1960s, strict adherence to the social script of transitions to adulthood began to unravel, as young people's entry into adulthood was deferred, first, by the Baby Boom generation and then by their children. Simultaneously, school success became *the* singular path to individual success that it is perceived to be today. With its emergence, the political implications of parents' disciplinary preferences ('authoritarianism' vs. 'permissiveness') faded in salience or were simply recast in the context of their relevance to school readiness debate (Colarco, 2014; Jones & Cox, 2012). Given the rise of authoritarian impulses across the world over the past several years, however, the political ramifications of parenting styles could very well regain the prominence it once enjoyed as the taproot of authoritarianism or democracy among observers of childrearing behavior.

Disclosure statement

No potential conflict of interest was reported by the author.

References

Adorno, T. W., Frenkel-Brunswick, E., Levinson, D. J., & Sanford, R. N. (1969). *The authoritarian personality* (p. 387). New York, NY: W. W. Norton and Company Inc.

Arnett, J. J. (2000). Emerging adulthood: A theory of development from the late teens through the twenties. *American Psychologist, 55*, 469–480.

Bailyn, B. (1960). *Education in the making of American society: Needs and opportunities for study*. Williamsburg, VA: Institute for Early American Culture.

Baumrind, D. (1966). Effects of authoritative parental control on child behavior. *Child Development, 37*, 887–907.

Baumrind, D. (1971). Current patterns of parental authority. *Developmental Psychology, 4* (1, Part 2), 1–103.

Baym, N. (1978). *Women's fiction: A guide to novels by and about women in America, 1820–1870*. Ithaca, NY: Cornell University Press.

Becker, G. S. (1980). *Human capital*. Chicago, IL: University of Chicago Press.

Block, J. E. (2012). *Crucible of consent*. Cambridge, MA: Harvard University Press.

Bourdieu, P., & Passeron, J. (1990). *Reproduction in Education, Society, and Culture*. R. Nice (trans). Newbury Park, CA: Sage.

Brodhead, R. H. (1988). Sparing the rod: Discipline and fiction in antebellum America. *Representations, 21*, 67–96.

Bronfenbrenner, U. (1958). Socialization and social class through time and space. In E. E. Maccoby, T. M. Newcomb, & E. L. Hartley (Eds.), *Readings in social psychology* (pp. 400–425). New York, NY: Holt, Reinhart and Winston.

Brooks, D. (2001). The organization kid. *The Atlantic Magazine*. Retrieved from https://www.theatlantic.com/magazine/archive/2001/04/the-organization-kid/302164/

Brooks, D. (2016, September 20). Dignity and sadness in the working class. *New York Times*. Retrieved from http://www.nytimes.com/2016/09/20/opinion/dignity-and-sadness-in-the-working-class.html

Burawoy, M. (2012). Pedagogy of the oppressed: Freire meets Bourdieu. In K. von Holdt & M. Burawoy (Eds.), *Conversations with Bourdieu: The Johannesburg moment* (pp. 219–226). Johannesburg: Wits University Press.

Calarco, J. M. (2014). Coached for the classroom: Parents' cultural transmission and children's reproduction of educational inequalities. *American Sociological Review, 79*, 1015–1037.

Chao, R. K. (1994). Beyond parental control and authoritarian parenting style: Understanding Chinese parenting through the cultural notion of training. *Child Development, 65*, 1111–1119.

Chua, A. (2011). *Battle hymn of the tiger mother*. New York, NY: Penguin Press.

Centers, R. (1950). Social class identifications of American youth. *Journal of Personality, 18*, 290–302.

Criss, M. M., & Larzelere, R. E. (2013). Introduction. In R. E. Larzelere, A. S. Morris, & A. W. Harrist (Eds.), *Authoritative parenting: Synthesizing nurturance and discipline for optimal child development* (pp. 3–8). Washington, DC: American Psychological Association.

Davidson, C. N. (1986). *Revolution and the word: The rise of the novel in America*. New York, NY: Oxford University Press.

Demos, J. (1970). *A little commonwealth: Family life in Plymouth colony*. New York, NY: Oxford University Press.

Demos, J. (1982). The changing faces of fatherhood. In S. H. Cath, A. R. Gurwitt, & J. M. Ross (Eds.), *Father and child: Developmental and clinical perspectives* (pp. 425–445). Boston, MA: Little, Brown and Company.

Douglas, A. (1977). *The feminization of American culture*. New York, NY: Avon.

Fass, P. S. (2016). *The end of American childhood: A history of parenting from life on the frontier to the managed child*. Princeton, NJ: Princeton University Press.

Fass, P. S., & Grossberg, M. (Eds.). (2012). *Reinventing childhood after world war II*. Philadelphia: University of Pennsylvania Press.

Fordham, S., & Ogbu, J. U. (1986). Black students' school success: Coping with the "burden of acting white". *The Urban Review, 18*, 176–206.

Fry, R. (2015). More millennials living with family despite improved job market. *Pew Research Center; Social and Demographic Trends*. Retrieved from http://www.pewsocialtrends.org/2015/07/29/more-millennials-living-with-family-despite-improved-job-market/

Gardner, H. (1983). *Frames of mind: The theory of multiple intelligences*. New York, NY: Basic Books.

Graebner, W. (1990). *Coming of age in Buffalo: Youth and authority in the postwar era*. Philadelphia, PA: Temple University Press.

Grant, J. (2014). *The boy problem: Educating boys in urban America, 1870–1970*. Baltimore: The Johns Hopkins University Press.

Hanisch, C. (1970). The personal is political. In S. Firestone & A. Koedt (Eds.), *Notes from the second year: Women's liberation; major writing of the radical feminists*. New York, NY: Radical Feminism.

Hart, B., & Risley, T. R. (1995). *Meaningful differences in the everyday experience of young American children*. Baltimore, MD: Brookes.

Heclo, H. (2008). *On thinking institutionally* (fig. 2.1; pp. 18–22). New York, NY: Oxford University Press.

Hill, C. (1964). The spiritualization of the household. In *Society and puritanism in pre-revolutionary England* (pp. 458–465). New York, NY: Schocken Books.

Hochschild, A. R. (1983). *The managed heart: Commercialization of human feeling*. Berkeley: University of California Press.

Hulbert, A. (2003). *Raising America: Experts, parents and a century of advice about children*. New York, NY: Vintage Books.

Isenberg, N. (2016). *White trash: The 400 year untold history of class in America*. New York, NY: Viking Press.

Jones, R. P., & Cox, D. (2012). *Beyond guns and god: The complexities of the white working class in America* (pp. 16–17). Washington, DC: The Public Religion Research Institute. Retrieved from http://www.prri.org/wp-content/uploads/2012/09/WWC-Report-For-Web-Final-1.pdf

Kessen, W. (1966). American psychology just before piaget. *Psychological Science, 7*, 196–199.

Kohn, M. L. (1969). *Class and conformity: A study in values*. Homewood, IL: The Dorsey Press.

Lassonde, S. (2005). *Learning to forget: Schooling and family life in New Haven's working class*. New Haven, CT: Yale University Press.

Lynd, R. S., & Lynd, H. M. (1929). *Middletown: A study in modern American culture*. New York, NY: Harcourt, Brace and Company.

Lynd, R. S., & Lynd, H. M. (1937). *Middletown in transition: A study in social conflicts*. New York, NY: Harcourt, Brace and Co.

Maccoby, E. E. (1992). The role of parents in the socialization of children: An historical overview. *Developmental Psychology, 28*, 1006–1017.

Marwick, A. (1998). *The sixties: Cultural revolution in Britain, France, Italy, and the United States, 1958–1974*. New York, NY: Oxford University Press.

Milkie, M., & Denny, K. E. (2013). Changes in the cultural model of father involvement. *Journal of Family Issues, 35*, 223–253.

Modell, J. (1989). *Into one's own: From youth to adulthood in the United States, 1920–1975*. Berkeley: University of California Press.

Morgan, Edmund, S. (1944). *The Puritan Family: Essays on Religion and Domestic Relations in Seventeenth-Century New England*. Boston: Trustees of the Public Library.

Nye, J. (1990). *Bound to lead: The changing nature of American power*. New York, NY: Basic Books.

Pew Research Center. (2016). For the first time in modern era, living with parents edges out other living arrangements for 18-34-year-olds: Shared living with spouse or partner continues to fall. *Pew Research Center; Social & Demographic Trends*. Retrieved from http://www.pewsocialtrends.org/2016/05/24/for-first-time-in-modern-era-living-with-parents-edges-out-other-living-arrangements-for-18-to-34-year-olds/

Pleck, J. H. (2007). Why could father involvement benefit children? Theoretical perspectives *Applied Development Science, 11*, 196–202.

Rubin, L. B. (1976). *Worlds of pain: Life in the working-class family*. New York, NY: Basic Books.

Ryan, M. P. (1981). *Cradle of the middle class: The family in Oneida, New York, 1790–1865* (pp. 157–161). Cambridge: Cambridge University Press.

Salovey, P., & Mayer, J. D. (1989). Emotional intelligence. *Imagination, Cognition and Personality, 9*, 185–211.

Shurtleff, N. B. (Ed.) (1853). Instructions for the punishment of incorrigible children. Reprinted in S. Cohen (Ed.) (1974) *Education in the United States: A documentary history* (Vol. 1, pp. 370). New York, NY: Random House.

Sklar, K. K. (1973). *Catherine beecher: A study in American domesticity*. New Haven, CT: Yale University Press.

Stearns, P. N. (2003). *Anxious parents: A history of modern childrearing in America*. New York: New York University Press.

Strickland, C. E., & Ambrose, A. M. (1985). The baby boom, prosperity, and the changing worlds of children, 1945–53. In J. M. Hawes & N. R. Hiner (Eds.), *American childhood: A research and historical handbook* (pp. 533–585). Westport, CT: Greenwood Press.

Tompkins, J. P. (1985). *Sensational designs: The cultural work of American fiction, 1790–1860*. New York, NY: Oxford University Press.

Vicedo, M. (2013). *The nature and nurture of love: From imprinting to attachment in cold war America* (p. 40). Chicago, NY: University of Chicago Press.

Warner, W. L., & Srole, L. (1945). *The social systems of American ethnic groups*. New Haven, CT: Yale University Press.

Wihbey, J. (2011). USDA report: Expenditures on children by families, 2010. *Journalist's Resource*, Shorenstein Center, Harvard Kennedy School. Retrieved from http://journalistsresource.org/studies/economics/personal-finance/expenditures-children-families-2010

Zelizer, V. (2005). The priceless child revisited. In J. Qvortrup (Ed.), *Studies in Modern Childhood: Society, Agency, Culture* (pp. 184–200). Basingstoke: Palgrave Macmillan.

The parent: A cultural invention. The politics of parenting*

Bengt Sandin

ABSTRACT

The welfare state interventionist position vis-à-vis families in Sweden during the twentieth century was justified by claims of parental incompetence and children's need for protection. Childhood was regarded as a period of growing but simultaneously a period with social rights. The development of government responsibility in support of parenting during the twentieth century reflected such an understanding of childhood. In social policy children were addressed as individual agents in the family. As a consequence, the competent child was discovered, and the need for government support of parents was cast in a new light. The need to develop parental competence became a focal point of government educational initiatives/programs at the same time as children were viewed as human moral models. Children were ascribed agency and competence with adult-like rights while the role of the welfare state scaled down in the wake of economic crises. This new imagery was underwritten by international conventions in the definition of childhood.

Introduction

The Swedish feminist writer Ellen Key became an international celebrity by arguing that the twentieth century would become 'the century of the child' at a time that coincided with the rise and development of the child-saving movement throughout the western world (Key, 1995). The concept originated in a play about family relations by the feminist Swedish playwright Frida Stéenhoff. For Stéenhoff the liberation of women from dependence on the family necessitated an increased commitment of the government for children in care and schooling; the liberation of children from the family was necessary for the emancipation of women. Contrary to Stéenhoff, Ellen Key emphasized mothering and was

*Article is based on a paper originally presented at the workshop: *Historical Perspectives on Child Development: Implications for Future Research*, Ann Arbor, May 12–14, 2016.

hesitant about the stifling influence of institutional arrangements in the life of children such as schools and kindergartens. Their views reflect different understandings of the family – and indeed the role of parents in the life of children. Ellen Key was a feminist and a central actor in the suffragette-movement in Sweden. However, she did not oppose the basic division of gender roles in the bourgeois family. For her the mother and family care was a key to the development of a society that was good for children. Stéenhoff's position suggests that the role of parents could be balanced by a government acting in loci parentis in the support of inadequate or absent parents (Carlsson Wetterberg, 2010). Both were ardent suffragettes and strong advocates for social reforms for children – fostering, child labour, and education – but their solutions were contrary to each other. The betterment of children's lives and social rights could to be achieved either through improved mothering (parenting) or through state intervention to protect children.

Studies of cultural systems around the world show that Sweden today holds an extreme position as an individualistic and modernistic society that sets it apart from societies in which traditional values, religion and family play larger roles. Interestingly, this individualism accepts and trusts government intervention in social matters (Berggren & Trägårdh, 2006; Trägårdh, 2007) but does it also downplay the role of family and family care? As several scholars have noted, interventions by government carry evidence of how parenting and family are defined and influence the parameters within which the development of children are understood (Andresen, 2011; Ohlander, 1993; Qvotrup, 2005; Sandin & Halldén, 2003; Therborn, 1993). In this article I will scrutinize the understanding of the parent as a historical and cultural archetype in Sweden, against the backdrop of the two alternatives represented by Key and Stéenhoff. I will point to a couple of fundamental aspects in the invention of the parent in the Swedish historical experience that also are related to how child development is politically framed, and how childhood is constructed. This article focuses on the pertinent, enduring, ubiquitous question: Can parents be trusted to manage the moral, physical and intellectual care of their children?

The parent, an institution, and a legacy – The context

The nation in which Frida Stéenhoff and Ellen Key expressed their thoughts on family, parents and the position of children was marked by a historical legacy that was signified by the questioning of parental abilities. The Lutheran church thus developed its traditions around the need to reach each individual with religious instructions. Educational reformers aimed at improving the social conditions of the working classes during the nineteenth century also viewed parent's abilities, as parents, critically as did the philanthropic associations that founded orphanages, schools and welfare agencies to support women and children. After the beginning of the twentieth century the Swedish state began to extend its responsibility over welfare arrangements and adopted similar attitudes to parent's capacities. As a corollary, the discussions about parents was also mirrored in the understanding of childhood.

The long tradition of intervention and support of family and parenting also transformed the understanding of childhood and child development. Particularly mothers were objects of reform and support in their role as mothers. This was much in the tradition expressed by Ellen Key but it did also reflex the vision expressed by Frida Stéenhoff for whom the state had a distinct role to play to make possible the liberation of women.

A set of laws dealing with delinquency, fostering and adoption, passed during the two first centuries, laid down the framework for the protection, punishment, and regulation of children that underwrote such a responsibility. These ideas also encompassed protection of society, and thus drew a fine line between protection and punishment (Gullberg, 2004; Jönson, 1997; Lindgren, 2006; Münger, 2000; Sundkvist, 1994). A government agency, the Child Guardians, was established in the 1920s to replace absent parents and to seek out fathers who did not pay for their children (Bergman, 2003).

As the state developed its ambitions to support families, it had to confront the fact that central government had only a relatively limited authority over a number of policies that were dealt with by either welfare boards in the local communities or by private institutions for children (Sköld, 2006; Sköld, Söderlind, & Bergman, 2014). Government policies and authority had to be, and were, therefore, developed, extending into the social and economic spheres of such institutions. In that process it was also necessary to define for example how fostering as well adoption were to be dealt with. Up until the beginning of the twentieth century these practices of creating families had been primarily dealt with through informal arrangements, but now the terms had to be defined by national legislation. Discussions, therefore, took place in parliament and in government commissions about the range of relevant issues inheritance, educational responsibilities, the best interest of the child, sibling relations, revoking or actualizing notions of parenting, and the ideal parent (Lindgren, 2006; Sköld, Söderlind, & Bergman, 2014). Public debate also focused the possible link between the large number of illegitimate children, child labour, working mothers, instable working class families and urban slums and the possible link to increasing crime rates. The role of government in the creation of a sustainable social contract had consequences for how the government defined the appropriate role and nature of parenting. But was it Ellen Key's or Freda Stéenhoff's vision of a century of the child that was realized in Sweden?

Welfare and the transformation of childhood

Under the Social Democratic government general welfare provisions for children were developed during the 1940s in Sweden, and the romantic notion of childhood became associated with the ambitions of the welfare state (Sandin & Halldén, 2003). The state addressed the needs of children through institutions and professionals who drew their legitimacy from the fact that they represented either local or central governments. A government publication issued in 1942, *Svenska Barn i Bild (Images of Swedish Children)* (Palmær, 1942), popularizing government child and family policies, illustrates precisely how children's rights were conceptualized as protected and embraced by the state in its attempt to meet the government's goals for population and health policies. The organization of welfare at state and local levels was described in some detail; the contribution made by foundations and philanthropic organizations is also recognized. Under the motto 'more children of better quality,' the authors of the publication declared that better, more coherent cooperation would ensure long-term excellence in childcare (Palmaer, introductory chapter). Pictures show institutions and welfare provisions, childcare professionals rather than parents, examples of order, control, supervision, inspection, good health and care, and children under the gaze of the professionals. An image of a child on a wooden horse, intertextually referring to the statues of kings on Swedish city centers, associated the child with both current national values and links him to an historical ideal (Palmær, 1942; Sandin & Sundkvist, 2014).

The notion of childhood as a vulnerable period that necessitates public institutions supported educational thinking and reform during the mid-twentieth century. The well-known Swedish educator Torsten Husén argued in the 1950s that children had little contact with adults either inside or outside the family. The nuclear family was regarded as a fragile construction. The failings of the family's social network, with one- and two-parent families, necessitated an expansion of public institutions. Since more mothers worked, latchkey children, who were not met by adults when they came home from school, became a source of new concern (Husén, 1987, pp. 12–14).

The dependence on professionally run institutions was a logical consequence of such ideas and in many political contexts was used to motivate the expansion of institutions. As an important consequence the influence of the British psychiatrist John Bowlby, who theorized about the emotional bond between mother and child, had very limited influence in Sweden in the 1950s and 1960s. Swedish psychologists and psychiatrists resisted his emphasis on the attachment between mother and children, arguing for more modern, institutional solutions to family problems (Broberg, 2006; Zetterqvist, 2009). Before the WW II, institutional solutions were tethered to the impoverished state of working families, but even as economic standards improved throughout Sweden, such solutions became even more widespread. The pattern of change indicates that families also saw such government help in the form of kindergartens and daycares facilities as preferable to placing children in foster care. Institutions that helped working and 'worn-out' mothers expanded during the 1950s, as did child guidance clinics, which before the war had been closely associated with disciplining school children, but now gained acceptance among parents. In the same spirit child psychiatry disassociated itself from the criminal justice system and social services and established a professional identity with a focus on individual therapeutic treatment (Jönson, 1997; Zetterqvist, 2009; Zetterqvist & Sandin, 2013). The expansion of the welfare system in this way gained legitimacy because it also offered tangible support: free school lunches (1947), family allowances (from 1949), and inexpensive medical care. Support was sometimes tied to measures aimed at shaping certain modes of behavior, and educational efforts aimed at forming particular attitudes toward child rearing and adult behavior, were identifiable in the maternity and child welfare centers (Gullberg, 2004; Sandin, 2012b). In the 1960s the need for public daycare was also clearly cast in the light of what was viewed as the problem of leaving children in the sole care of parents. The danger of long-lasting psychological damage was considered imminent if children were left only to parents. Educated personnel could therefore mitigate the negative consequences of parenting. The helplessness of children and their dependence on professionals were emphasized in for example the views of a government commission on childcare. Public child care had the potential to alleviate the dangers of otherwise associated with upbringing in the care of parents.

> Psychology and child psychiatry have taught us how early disturbances can continue through many years with changed symptoms. Damage of a serious nature during the first years of life can continue as contact difficulties and aggression among pre-school children, as discipline and learning problems among school-children, and as asocial behaviour and criminality among adolescents; it can also lead to disease of psychophysical type among adults. This is one of our most powerful and noticeable chain reactions. Behavioural science has shown that many personality disorders, character disturbances, and illnesses are due to unsatisfactory emotional conditions during our long, helpless childhood, when personality and character are established. Barnstugor, Barnavårdsmannaskap, Barnolycksfall. (SOU 1967:8, p. 46)

Schooling for all and the integrity and rights of children

During the 1950s Sweden was at last ready to create a school system for all social classes, a comprehensive school (*bottenskola*) much influenced by American educational ideas. The vision of a school for all included curricular reform and new pedagogical ideas, as well as the creation of a unified national school system, that undermined the existing system with different schools for different social classes and gender *(parallellskola)*. Importantly, it also changed the understanding of children's rights and legal protection. The high school (*läroverket)* and the elementary school (*folkskola*) permitted different ways of disciplining children, which also reflected the social makeup of the schools. Corporal punishment had been allowed in the elementary schools, but it was banned in the high schools. The merging of the schools led to a reevaluation of the system of discipline, ending with a ban on corporal punishment as early as in 1957. The argument was of a democratic and developmental nature: physical punishment created fascist and authoritarian personalities in the adult. Henceforth, discipline in the educational system would use methods adopted from psychology in accordance with children's developmental trajectories rather than physical punishment (Qvarsebo, 2006; Sandin, 2012a).

The important consequence was that, in the process children were given the same rights as adults regarding the integrity of their bodies, thus transcending, in a manner of speaking, the traditional limits of childhood which to that point had not included bodily (or mental) protection. Moreover, this ban marked the beginning of a discussion about children's integrity in terms that were taken even further in the late 1960s. A ban on parents' rights to physically discipline children, implemented in 1979, was included in the family law code (Schiratzki, 2006; Singer, 2000). Such understanding was also founded on a conceptualization of children's development and the effect of physical humiliation on the psyche and their development. The government developed social policies that displayed its intent to protect the individual child and also to mandate proper childrearing practices. This became increasingly clear in the debates in the 1970 around childcare and the necessity that men and women were equally engaged parents, and shared the parental duties equally. The government responded then in support of feminist demands that families should also organize themselves around principles of gender equality among children. It was clear that the childcare and family policy and parental support systems was construed on the expectation that families should adhere to the norms of behavior outlined in the new policies (Klinth, 1999; Schiratzki 2008, pp. 46–52). An important cultural undercurrent is the trust in the state as guarantor of freedom and a supporter of individual choices in Sweden. The system of regulation of family and parenting was largely done with the consent of popular attitudes. The state and government regulation represented freedom and positive support in Swedish popular and political understandings. Commercialization and the market are commonly understood as restricting individuals (marked by age, social class or gender) from expressing or realizing life projects, whereas the state guarantees freedom from such economic and social limitations (Svallfors, 1996; Berggren & Trägardh, 2006).

Parenting and the rights of children – an interdependent relationship

When the education system was reformed in 1947, the government also decided that families needed compensation for lost incomes and the increasing costs of bringing up the young, since children would spend a longer period in schools. This was compounded by the decision to finance free school meals for all children, which was introduced over a period of ten years. All families were given a family allowance, 'child support,' without individual evaluation of need (Betänkande, 1946; Sandin, 2012a). The symbolic meaning of child allowances, however, has changed significantly over the years. Children's wages earned outside the family were replaced, where families could afford it, by pocket money distributed by the family head, again a symbol of dependence within the family. But some forty years later, the government-issued child benefit is looked upon as the children's own money. It has become a symbol of adulthood – albeit within the family – and of trust in the children as independent consumers capable of planning their own consumption of clothing, cinema tickets, mobile phones and other amusements. The support is also an expression of the direct relationship between children and the state, of state-supported individualism (Näsman & Gerber, 2003; Sandin, 2012a; Söderlind & Engwall, 2008).

During the late 1970s the national educational system took on the responsibility of channeling children into 'suitable' leisure activities. This is in part an extension of the school's role as an institution for social policy, where preventive health care has also been crucial in complementing the role of parents Kulturutredningen (1995). The intervention by the state by economic and organizational means in supporting children's culture and appropriate leisure activities, reflected a critical attitude toward market solutions and, conversely, a trust that only the state could uphold diversity and quality of cultural offerings. This policy represented, in theory, an egalitarian distribution of resources and access to culture for children in culturally deprived environments (Kulturutredningen, 1995; Sandin & Halldén, 2003).

The idea that women could work and men could participate in child rearing gave extra urgency to demands for parental education and an expansion of day care. The new, equality-minded men were to be produced by means of information and education, and women entered the labor market in greater numbers (Johansson, 2004; Johansson & Klinth, 2007; Klinth, 1999, 2008). This also entails a changing understanding of the border between institutions of care and educational institutions. In 1990 responsibility for child care was transferred from the social welfare administration to the educational authorities. In the late 1990s the final year of child-care was redefined as a preparatory school year; it was not care but education (Halldén, 1988, 1992; Persson, 1998). The number of children placed in orphanages and foster care has also decreased as a publicly accessible and inexpensive day care system has since the 1960s made it possible for more single women and men to both care for their children and support themselves. More have the opportunity to live family life, thereby underwriting a broad definition of parenting. Social welfare institutions and public day care made it possible for single and poor parents to maintain their families (Nyberg, 2000, pp. 5–20; Sallnäs, 2000). At the same time the institutions changed the focus from care to educational progression.

The fact that fatherhood started to be defined as an emotional rather than an economic dilemma can also be understood in relation to the fact that single parents do not depend on contributions (family support) from the other parent. If child support is not paid by the absent parent, the local government social services will forward the money and charge the defaulting parent (Bergman, 2003; Forsberg, 2009; Sandin, 2012b). Thus in such cases the state creates the material bases for defining fatherhood primarily in relational terms.

Up to the 1960s, in the period when the welfare state was under construction, the strong position of the state relative to families was justified by referring the need of children for protection. The change in the understanding of children's rights that took place as a consequence of the ban on corporal punishment implies similarities with adults, not differences. In a manner of speaking, it makes void the differences between children and the older generation.

Children's rights are thus understood to be equivalent to those of adults, making children autonomous within the family – or at least not simply subsumed within it – and invested with the right to be respected as individuals with opinions, knowledge, emotions, and skills, and in possession of civil rights as citizens (Sandin, 2012b). This view presupposes a new kind of parenting, shared equally between the parents who are educationally aware, responsible, and knowledgeable about child needs, development, and rights as individuals.

The parliamentary committee from the 1970s that looked into the question of children's rights and that in due time also led to the legislation prohibiting abuse of children within the family, made a re-discovery. They viewed the attachment theory anew as an important and neglected baseline in Swedish social policy (Bengt Sandin ongoing research). It became an instrument in the debates that followed about children's rights, and motivated a larger emphasis on the need to educate parents. Developmental theory also underwrote the United Nations Convention on the Rights of the Child (UNCRC) and the work of the Barnombudsman in Norway, for example (Flekkøy, 1991; Flekköy & Kaufman, 1997). Since the late 1960s it has been argued in the parliament that parenting in families requires direct government support apart from the general welfare schemes, like comprehensive child care, free hospital and dental care etc. Parents need to be educated in the role of bringing up children. At start the emphases was on the care of small infants, organized by local child and mother health centers, but broaden during the 70s to include older children in programs run by local communities. It was a recurrent discussion in the parliament about that the incompetence and insecurity parents called for more direct educational programs which later on shift focus to emphasize that society be more accommodating to parenting. It is during this period child care institution expanded, allowing women to both work and be mothers but it also initiated a discussion about how well the modern society was allowing men and women to be good parents (Sandin, 2011).

Childhood and the transformation of welfare

A distinct change of course became evident in the 1990s with the formulation of a new system of governance of the welfare society. It was based on a larger degree of local self-rule and less emphasis on national standards and homogeneous systems of support and social provisions. Local and regional service providers were given a larger amount of autonomy in defining their roles. The state limited its role in children's evaluation and measurement to generally defined political aims (Sandin & Halldén, 2003). The emphasis shifted to the judicial system's responsibility to define children's rights in relationship to the 1989 UNCRC. The emphasis on children's autonomy, competence and independent agency also provided an opportunity for civil society and professional organizations to offer children support, protection, or legal advice in lieu of the guarantees previously afforded by the state. The child's best interests and participatory rights became a unifying concept that is enlisted by partially rival agents that at the same time represent and voice their professional interests (Flekköy & Kaufman, 1997; Rasmusson, 1994; Regeringens proposition, 1991).

Children's voices have created a novel understanding of a whole new spectrum of social and health problems and development among young people that is very similar to the problems affecting adults, including stress, anxiety, and work-related worries, underpinning the similarities between the young and adults (Kommittén, 2002; Zetterqvist, 2001). Competent children also need parents with matching skills. Significant is the concerted effort to create and support parental educational programs run by local communities, including those designed as therapeutic treatment. The parents' relational competencies and knowledge about children's development and rights are to be strengthened. When such programs are used as general welfare instruments for all children, the consequences are sometimes problematical. The emphasis tends to be on educating the parental generation in order to strengthen the family with professional and formal educational support rather than upholding well-functioning welfare institutions and the unemployment rates at a low level. The evaluation systems that reach parents with instruction arranged by schools, social services or parent organizations come in conflict with other professional agendas. Are teachers in schools to also teach parents, about children? It is clearly also a problem that programs developed for therapy in closed treatments are used as universal programs for the support of children and families. The emphases on the family, parenting and a less interventionist state brings us back to the conflict between Key and Stéenhoff that runs through the history. It is time again for a focus on the family and its internal relationship rather than public welfare institutions of support (Adamson & Bennett, 2008; Kvist Lindholm, 2015;

Löf, 2011; Sandin, 2011; Sandin & Bergnehr, 2013; http://www.fhi.se/sv/Aktuellt/Nyheter/50-miljoner-till-lokalt-folkhalsoarbete-for-barn-och-unga (11 April 2011), Ongoing research by Sofia Littmark, Univ of Linkoping).

In perspective

In the period when the welfare state was being constructed, the strong position of the state in relation to families was justified with reference to children's needs for protection and the parents' incompetence. This built on a long-standing tradition of intervention to support parenting. The religious traditions, educational system and a number of public health initiatives tended to intervene and regulate parents. The actions were founded on notions of the inadequate quality of the parenting, in traditional households, the working classes as well as single mothers. These, in turn, stimulated discussions about the normal development as well as different ways of describing normality, that was shaped by the development of a comprehensive system of schooling. In this process children and teenagers were also singled out as special social categories.

Children and teenagers were cast as either the romantic emotional child or troublesome adolescent. Childhood as a whole was a period of growing and incompetence to be overcome as soon as possible, but simultaneously a period with social rights. Government took on the responsibility in lieu of the parent (or support) through a number of initiatives, that spanned from economic support, child care, to guidance of children and a more inclusive school system. This transformed the notions of childhood. Children were described as autonomous and with adult-like rights and in social policy addressed as individuals in the family. The competent child was invented and discovered as a partner in collaboration with professionals. Its qualities were romanticized. Parallel to the description of children as moral and ethical paragons, the description of the distinctive nature of children was also reappraised, and the legislation increasingly emphasized children's competence and parity with adults in the question of rights. There was likeness rather than difference. This also highlights the question of children's simultaneous need for protection and care, and places emphasis on the need to re-evaluate parental competence as well. The need to develop parental competence became a focal point of government educational initiatives/programs at the same time as children were presented as human moral models. Yet, children were in need of protection and care to develop normally at the same time as they were ascribed agency and competence, and models for adults. The child is increasingly seen as a competent co-actor with the state and civil society, with the duties and responsibilities of the citizen, but also with the citizen's rights. The changed civic role of the child is also expressed through the changes in the law relevant to children and by creating a child ombudsman to represent the voice of children.

A distinct change of course is made clear in the formulation of a new system of governance from the late 1990s. The state is taking less detailed responsibility for shaping conditions for children. The negotiation between the old actors is now carried on with new elements in a partly different arena and with more participants. This has meant a new emphasis on a discussion of children's rights. 'The best interest of the child' has been held up as a goal for social-policy interventions and is defining the role of civil society organizations with support of a global convention. In essential respects the conditions are thus changed for interaction between state, professionals and children, as this also has to be negotiated in new political and social arenas in the welfare society.

Disclosure statement

No potential conflict of interest was reported by the author.

References

Adamson, P., & Bennett. (2008). *The child care transition: A league table of early childhood education and care in economically advanced countries* (Innocenti report card 8). Florence: UNICEF Innocenti Research Center.

Andresen, A. (2011). *Barnen och välfärdspolitiken. Nordiska barndomar 1900–2000* [Children and welfare policy. Nordic childhoods 1900–2000]. Stockholm: Dialogos förlag.

Berggren, H., & Trägårdh, L. (2006). *Är svensken människa?: gemenskap och oberoende i det moderna Sverige* [Are Swedes human? Community and independence in modern Sweden]. Stockholm: Norstedt.

Bergman, H. (2003). *Att fostra till föräldraskap: barnavårdsmän, genuspolitik och välfärdsstat 1900–1950* [Educating for parenthood: The child welfare officer, gender policy and the welfare state 1900–1950] (Diss.). Stockholm University, Stockholm.

Betänkande om barnkostnadernas fördelning med förslag angående allmänna barnbidrag m. m. (1946). *Bilagor, 1941 års befolkningsutredning* [The government report on the distribution of the costs of children with proposals concerning general child allowances, etc. Appendices. The 1941 population commission]. Stockholm: Allmänna förlaget.

Broberg, A. (2006). *Anknytningsteori: betydelsen av nära känslomässiga relationer* [Attachment theory: The meaning of close emotional relations] (1nd ed.). Stockholm: Natur och kultur

Carlsson Wetterberg, C. (1992). *Feminismen, moderskapet och kärleken: Frida Stéenhoff i sekelskiftets samhällsdebatt* [Feminism, motherhood and love: Frida Stéenhoff in the turn of the century social debate]. Historisk tidskrift. Stockholm. 112, s. [517]–538.

Carlsson Wetterberg, C. (2010). *-bara ett öfverskott af lif-: en biografi om Frida Stéenhoff (1865–1945)* [-just a little surplus life-: A biography of Frida Stéenhoff (1865–1945)]. Stockholm: Atlantis.

Flekkøy, M. G. (1991). *A voice for children: Speaking out as their ombudsman*. London: Kingsley.

Flekköy, M. G., & Kaufman, N. H. (1997). *The participation rights of the child: Rights and responsibilities in family and society*. London: Jessica Kingsley.

Forsberg, L. (2009). *Involved parenthood: Everyday lives of Swedish middle-class families*. Linköping: Linköping University.

Gullberg, E. (2004). *Det välnärda barnet: föreställningar och politik i skolmåltidens historia* [The well-nourished child: Notions and politics in the history of school meals]. Linköping: Linköping University.

Halldén, G. (1988). *Förhållandet till tid: en föräldragrupps reflektioner över utveckling och uppfostran* [The relationship to time: Reflections of a group of parents on development and child-raising]. Stockholm.

Halldén, G. (1992). *Föräldrars tankar om barn: uppfostringsideologi som kultur* [Parents thoughts on children: Ideologies of child-raising as culture]. Stockholm: Carlsson.

Husén, T. (1987). *Vad har hänt med skolan?: perspektiv på skolreformerna* (pp. 12–14). Stockholm: Verbum Gothia.

Johansson, T. (2004). *Faderskapets omvandlingar: frånvarons socialpsykologi* [Transforming fatherhood]. Göteborg: Daidalos.

Johansson, T., & Klinth, R. (2007). "De nya fäderna: om pappaledighet, jämställdhet och nya maskulina positioner" [The new fathers: On paternal parental leave, equal opportunities and new masculine positions]." *Tidskrift för genusvetenskap: konst—scen, film, forskning, 1, 2,* 143–166

Jönson, U. (1997). *Bråkiga, lösaktiga och nagelbitande barn: om barn och barnproblem vid en rådgivningsbyrå i Stockholm 1933–1950* [Unruly, promiscuous and nail-biting children: On children and the child problem at a counseling cemter in Stockholm 1033–1950]. Linköping: Linköping University.

Key, E. (1995). *Barnets århundrade* [The century of the child]. Stockholm: ABF.

Klinth, R. (1999). The man and the equal family: A study of the new images of masculinity in the educational radio and TV programmes in Sweden, 1946–1971. In R. Torstendahl (Ed.), *State policy and gender system in the two German states and Sweden, 1945–1989* (pp. 169–197). Uppsala: Historiska institutionen, Uppsala University.

Klinth, R. (2008, Winter). "The best of both worlds?" *Fathering, 6*: 34.

Kommittén Välfärdsbokslut and Palme. (2002). *The final accounts of welfare and Palme.* The committee on the, Welfare in Sweden.

Kulturutredningen. (1995). *Tjugo års kulturpolitik 1974–1994: en rapport från Kulturutredningen* [Twenty years of cultural policy: A report from the commission on culture]. Stockholm: Fritze.

Kvist Lindholm, S. (2015). *The Paradoxes of Socio-Emotional Programmes in School: Young people's perspectives and public health discourses* (Diss. (sammanfattning)). Linköping: Linköpings universitet.

Lindgren, C. (2006). *En riktig familj: adoption, föräldraskap och barnets bästa 1917–1975* [A real family: Adoption, parenthood and the best interests of the child] (Diss.). Linköping: Linköpings universitet. Stockholm.

Löf, C. (2011). *Med livet på schemat: om skolämnet livskunskap och den riskfyllda barndomen* [With life on the schedule: On the school subject life competencies and a childhood full of risks] (PhD diss.). Lund: Lund Universitet.

Münger, A.-C. (2000). *Stadens barn på landet: Stockholms sommarlovskolonier och den moderna välfärden* [Ctiy children in the country: Stockholm's summer vacation camps and modern welfare]. Linköping: Linköping University.

Näsman, E., & Gerber, C. V. (2003). *Från spargris till kontokort: barndomens ekonomiska spiraltrappa* [From piggy bank to credit card: The spiral staircase of childhood]. Norrköping: Institutionen för tematisk utbildning och forskning, Linköpings Universitet.

Nyberg, A. (2000). From foster mothers to child care centers: A history of working mothers and child care in Sweden. *Feminist Economics, 6,* 5–20.

Ohlander, A.-S. (1993). *Det bortträngda barnet: uppsatser om psykoanalys och historia* [Pushing children aside: Essays on psychoanalysis and history]. Uppsala: Historiska institutionen.

Palmær, M. (1942). *Svenska Barn i Bild* [Images of Swedish children]. Stockholm: Redaktionskommittén for Svenska Barn i Bild.

Persson, S. (1998). *Förskolan i ett samhällsperspektiv*. Lund: Studentlitteratur.

Qvarsebo, J. (2006). *Skolbarnets fostran: enhetsskolan, agan och politiken om barnet 1946–1962* [The fostering of school children: The common school, physical punishment and policies on children 1946–1962]. Linköping: Linköping University.

Qvotrup, J. (2005). Varieties of childhood. In J. Qvotrup (Ed.), *Studies in modern childhood, society, agency, culture*. London: Palgrave Macmillan.

Rasmusson, B. (1994). *Barnperspektiv: Reflektioner kring ett mångtydigt och föränderligt begrepp* [The child's perspective: Reflections on an ambiguous and changing concept]. Stockholm: Barnombudsmannen.

Regeringens proposition 1997/98:182 Strategi för förverkligande av FN:s konvention om barnets rättigheter i Sverige. Stockholm: Socialdepartementet Statens Offentliga Utredningar, 1991: 70, 23.

Retrieved April 11, 2011, from http://www.fhi.se/sv/Aktuellt/Nyheter/50-miljoner-till-lokalt-folkhalsoarbete-for-barn-och-unga

Sallnäs, M. (2000). *Barnavårdens institutioner: framväxt, ideologi och strukture* [Child care institutions: Growth, ideology and structure]. Stockholm: Stockholm University.

Sandin, B. (2011). *Föräldraskap - en arena för förhandling om barndomens innebörder. Ett historiskt perspektiv diskussionen om föräldraskap* [Parenthood – An arena for the negotiation of the meanings childhood: A discussion on parenthood from a historical perspective]. Stockholm: Locus.

Sandin, B. (2012a). 'More children of better quality': Pricing the child in the welfare state. In A. Sparrman, B. Sandin, & J. Sjöberg (Eds.), *Situating child consumption: Rethinking values and notions of children, childhood and consumption* (pp. 61–79). Lund: Nordic Academic Press.

Sandin, B. (2012b). Children and the swedish welfare state: From different to similar. In *Reinventing childhood after World War II*. (S. 110–138).

Sandin, B., & Halldén, G. (Eds.). (2003). *Barnets bästa: en antologi om barndomens innebörder och välfärdens organisering* [The best interests of the child: An anthology on the meanings of childhood and the organization of welfare]. Eslöv: B. Östlings bokförlag Symposion.

Sandin, B., & Bergnéhr, D. (2013). *Samverkande föräldrastöd* [Cooperation in parent support] Linköping: Linköping University Electronic Press.

Sandin, B., & Sundkvist, M. (2014). *Barn, barndom och samhälle: svensk utbildningshistoria* [Children, childhood and society: Swedish educational history] (1. uppl.). Malmö: Gleerup.

Schiratzki, J. (2006). *Barnrättens grunder* [The foundation of children's rights]. Lund: Studentlitteratur.

Schiratzki, J. (2008). *Mamma och pappa inför rätta* [Mamma and pappa in court] (pp. 46–52). Uppsala: Iustus.

Singer, A. (2000). *Föräldraskap i rättslig belysning* [Parenthood as seen in the law]. Uppsala University.

Sköld, J. (2006). *Fosterbarnsindustri eller människokärlek: barn, familjer och utackorderingsbyrån i Stockholm 1890–1925* [The foster child industry or human love: Children, families and the bureau for boarding out children in Stockholm 1890–1925] (Diss.). Stockholm: Stockholms universitet.

Sköld, J., Söderlind, I., & Bergman, A. (2014). *Fosterbarn i tid och rum: lokal och regional variation i svensk fosterbarnsvård ca 1850–2000* [Foster children in time and space: Local and regional variations in Swedish foster care ca 1850–2000]. Stockholm: Carlsson.

Söderlind, I., & Engwall, K. (Eds.). (2008). *Barndom och arbete* [Childhood and work]. Umeå: Boréa, chap. 7.
Statens kulturråd. (1997). *Kulturpolitik i praktiken: statliga kulturinsatser: en översikt*, 9. Stockholm: Statens kulturråd.
Sundkvist, M. (1994). *De vanartade barnen: mötet mellan barn, föräldrar och Norrköpings barnavårdsnämnd 1903–1925* (PhD diss.). Linköping: Linköping Universitet.
Svallfors, S. (1996). *Välfärdsstatens moraliska ekonomi: välfärdsopinionen i 90-talets Sverige* [The moral economy of the welfare state: Opinionc on welfare in Sweden in the 1990s] (1. uppl.). Umeå: Boréa.
Trägårdh, L. (2007). The 'civil society' debate in Sweden: The welfare state challenged. In L. Trägårdh (Ed.), *State and civil society in Northern Europe: The Swedish model reconsidered* (pp. 9–36). New York, NY: Berghahn.
Zetterqvist, N. K. (2001). *Att mäta barns psykiska hälsa med självskattningsenkäter: en kunskapsöversikt* [Measuring the mental health of children with self-evaluation forms: A survey]. Linköping: Folkhälsovetenskapligt centrum.
Zetterqvist, N. K. (2009). "När Bowlby kom till Sverige. Från motstånd till erkännande: anknytningsteori i Sverige 1950–2000." In A.-M. Markström, M. Simonsson, I. Söderlind, & E. Änggård (Eds.), *Barn, barndom och föräldraskap*. ns, 271–290. Stockholm: Carlssons.
Zetterqvist, N. K., & Sandin, B. (2013). Psychodynamics in child psychiatry in Sweden: From political vision to treatment ideology, 1945–1985. *History of Psychiatry, 24*, 308–325.

Index

Note: Boldface pagenumbers refer to tables & italic pagenumbers refer to figures.

For Product Safety Concerns and Information please contact our EU representative GPSR@taylorandfrancis.com
Taylor & Francis Verlag GmbH, Kaufingerstraße 24, 80331 München, Germany

www.ingramcontent.com/pod-product-compliance
Ingram Content Group UK Ltd.
Pitfield, Milton Keynes, MK11 3LW, UK
UKHW011019180926
475701UK00004B/826
* 9 7 8 0 3 6 7 5 8 2 9 0 6 *